D1478569

ADHD on Trial

ADHD on Trial

Courtroom Clashes over the Meaning of "Disability"

MICHAEL GORDON, Ph.D.

Westport, Connecticut
London

Library of Congress Cataloging-in-Publication Data

Gordon, Michael, Ph.D.
  ADHD on trial : courtroom clashes over the meaning of
"disability" / Michael Gordon.
    p. cm.
  Includes bibliographical references and index.
  ISBN 978-0-313-36015-2 (alk. paper)
  1. Love, Jonathan M.—Trials, litigation, etc. 2. Law School Admission
Council—Trials, litigation, etc. 3. Law schools—United States—
Entrance examinations. 4. Attention-deficit hyperactivity disorder—
Law and legislation—United States. 5. Disability evaluation—
United States. I. Title.
  KF228.L686G67 2009
  346.7301'3—dc22   2008040395

British Library Cataloguing in Publication Data is available.

Library of Congress Catalog Card Number: 2008040395
ISBN: 978-0-313-36015-2

First published in 2009

Praeger Publishers, 88 Post Road West, Westport, CT 06881
An imprint of Greenwood Publishing Group, Inc.
www.praeger.com

Printed in the United States of America

The paper used in this book complies with the
Permanent Paper Standard issued by the National
Information Standards Organization (Z39.48–1984).

10 9 8 7 6 5 4 3 2 1

To Americans with bona fide disabilities and those who provide them care.

Contents

Acknowledgments

Since I began writing this book, I maintained a list of friends and colleagues I wanted to thank for their input and support. The length of that inventory serves as a powerful testament to my good fortune. I have learned much over the years from fellow ADA consultants Kevin Murphy, David Damari, John Ranseen, George Litchford, Marla Brassard, Dawn Flanagan, Gerald Golden, Joe Bernier, and Samuel Ortiz. A cadre of administrators and lawyers involved with test accommodations has been unusually patient through the years in responding to my ceaseless barrage of questions and challenges. They include Shelby Keiser, Janet Carson, Elizabeth Azari, Shelley Green, Suzanne Williams, Catherine Farmer, John McAlary, Joan VanTol, Kim Dempsey, Gayle Murphy, Charles Meyer, Bob Burgoyne, and Bruce Eddington.

I thank Mantosh Dewan for allowing me the time to write this book and for being the kind of Department Chair that most academic faculty in this world can only dream about. Kevin Antshel, Sam Goldstein, Jud Staller, and Russell Barkley each offered help and encouragement along the way as did my local support crew comprising Sandy Stowell and Jennifer Rheinheimer. A cadre of friends also contributed in their own fashion, often by serving as sounding boards or offering productive opportunities to escape from laptop enslavement. They include Michael Calo, Bob Nelkin, Chuck Davoli, and Klaas Schilder.

As always, my wife, Wendy, served as a steady support and an enthusiastic reader. My in-family legal team comprised of son, Alex, and daughter-in-law, Lucy, provided access to Nexus/Lexis and a willingness to check the manuscript for legal accuracy.

I owe a singular debt of gratitude to Jane Leopold-Leventhal and Grace Deon of the Eastburn & Gray law firm. They were abundantly kind and encouraging throughout the litigation and have been enormously helpful to me since that time (in no small part by offering up the services of their able assistant, Lori French). More importantly, they exhibited a level of skill, determination, and good humor that was truly inspirational.

Finally, I want to thank three people who have been unwavering in their direct contributions to the manuscript, not to mention the quality of my life more generally. Ben Lovett, former graduate student but now valued colleague, let me pick his prodigious brain without complaint. His encyclopedic knowledge of the scientific literature made easy work of library research. My dear friend and colleague, Larry Lewandowski, has been a remarkable collaborator, editor, and source of wisdom for many years. His input and insights suffuse this book. And son Joshua, despite his relative youth and busy schedule, has proven himself an astute editor. He has also served as a one-man technical and spiritual support team, perhaps more than he may even realize.

CHAPTER 1
The Review

In the witness chair of Courtroom 8A of the United States Federal Courthouse in Philadelphia, Pennsylvania, sat Jonathan M. Love, twenty-five years old, dark-haired, handsome, and of earnest demeanor. Above and to his right, Judge R. Barclay Surrick remained hunched in his worn leather chair, filling a seventh yellow legal pad with notes, stopping occasionally to glance toward the well-spoken witness. Directly below, the court reporter stared at his monitor, interrupting his gaze only to type an identifier into the voice recognition system that recorded these proceedings. The last inhabitant of the judge's segmented throne was a young law clerk, Rachel Goldfarb, destined to write the first draft of Judge Surrick's ultimate decision in the case of *Jonathan Love* v. *the Law School Admission Council (LSAC)*.

The trial, in its third day, had already consumed the energies, talents, and monies of a small army of lawyers, paralegals, clerks, video technicians, transcriptionists, legal reporters, secretaries, consultants, and expert witnesses like me. Along each long wall of the dark-paneled courtroom the lawyers for both sides had lined box upon box of documents, all carefully tabbed and catalogued. The counsel tables were festooned with yellow legal pads, brown accordion files, and white binders that sprouted even more sheets of paper. A technician hired by the defense sat before two laptops, an LCD projector, a portable scanner, and his own assortment of indexes and notebooks. Contained within these assorted bins, files, and digital storage media were transcripts of twelve depositions, at least as many declarations, a collection of legal filings and affidavits, psychological test evaluation reports, trial notes, and memoranda. Mr. Love's quest had generated no less than seven thousand pages of documents.

This outflow of resources began four months earlier when Charles Weiner, Esquire, on behalf of Mr. Love and the Disability Rights Advocates of Berkley, California, filed suit in federal court for the Eastern District of Pennsylvania. That document entitled, "Complaint for the Violation of Civil Rights: The Americans with Disabilities Act of 1990; Request for Declaratory and Injunctive Relief," alleged that the LSAC had violated Mr. Love's civil rights. Just fourteen pages long, it was the trigger on the Gatling gun of legal ammunition that sprayed the tables and floors of Judge Surrick's court.

Mr. Love's legal challenge against the LSAC was born of his opinion that they had unlawfully denied him extra time to take the LSAT, the Law School Admission Test. The LSAC administers this examination, the equivalent of the Scholastic Assessment Test (SAT) or American College Test (ACT) for college admissions, four times per year to approximately 140,000 prospective law school applicants. It was Jonathan's contention that his disability, Attention Deficit Hyperactivity Disorder, entitled him to the accommodations that the LSAC had repeatedly denied. He pursued legal action to force the LSAC to permit him to take the test in a manner that would allow him to achieve a score unfettered by the impact of his purported disability.

The LSAC had other ideas. They considered Jonathan Love unqualified as disabled as defined by the Americans with Disabilities Act (ADA). From their perspective, no evidence existed that he had ADHD or any other psychiatric disorder. Furthermore, they contended that, even if he had a psychiatric disorder, it did not substantially impair his capacity to take their test.

The issues that swirl around this single case have proven striking for their number, complexity, and relevance to the lives of individuals with disabilities and those who consider themselves as such perhaps as a basis for gaining advantage. It poses a dizzying array of questions to clinicians, researchers, lawyers, disabilities specialists, professional licensing agencies, and testing organizations: What constitutes a psychiatric disorder as opposed to a normal variation in abilities or personality? When does unevenness in an individual's matrix of aptitudes and skills become pathological? What is the distinction between a psychiatric definition of a disorder and a legal definition of disability? Are there downsides to lowering thresholds for what constitutes a disorder/disability? What are the circumstances that might justify considering someone as both "high functioning" yet disabled? Was the ADA intended to encompass those who have functioned well, but perhaps not as well as they would have liked or up to what they perceive as their potential? How do you assess someone's "potential?" Does measured IQ serve as a proper marker? If not, what are reliable predictors? When does deference to an individual with a disability begin to invade the rights of the nondisabled? Should someone who wants to become a lawyer or doctor be entitled to accommodations that guarantee that outcome? At what point does accommodating an individual with a disability represent a risk to self or others?

Questions also abound about the process by which professionals assess psychiatric disorders generally and ADHD in particular. What are the diagnostic criteria for ADHD? Can a person have ADHD even though he has no childhood history of hyperactivity, impulsiveness, or inattention? Can someone with severe ADHD graduate from a four-year college without any special accommodations or regular treatment with medication? What should be the qualifications for someone who evaluates an individual for a psychiatric disorder? To what degree is it reasonable to rely on a person's self-report when he has a desired outcome? For someone with ADHD or a learning disability, what's the impact of extra time on their scores? Is extended time a fair and reasonable accommodation?

My personal involvement began innocently enough when an e-mail arrived from Dr. Kim Dempsey of the LSAC on July 31, 2006. The message contained two attachments, both Portable Document Format (PDF) files, with scanned copies of the documentation Jonathan had submitted. Dr. Dempsey, a clinical neuropsychologist by training, heads up the "Accommodated Testing Unit" at the LSAC. Her responsibility is to oversee the documentation review process, no small task given the roughly 1,500 cases that cross her desk every year. She is one of the many professionals whose job was created as a consequence of the law's passage. Indeed, the ADA has been a kind of public works program for legions of psychologists, psychiatrists, learning disabilities specialists, administrators, disabilities consultants, and lawyers who have found the ADA good for the bottom line. The law has created a nationwide industry dedicated to ensuring that individuals seeking ADA-type accommodations are dealt with legally.

Mr. Love first requested the accommodation of extra time on the LSAT in October 2004, having taken the exam under standard conditions the prior year. Following guidelines posted on the LSAC Web site, he submitted psychological reports and other records, all of which landed on Dr. Dempsey's desk. According to court records, she reviewed the information and determined that it did not support the claim for an accommodation. In a letter to Mr. Love dated November 3, 2004, she wrote that the "documentation provided does not demonstrate a substantial limitation related to taking the LSAT." After some additional correspondence, Mr. Love paused in his quest regarding the LSAT, applying instead for accommodations on the Graduate Management Admission Test (GMAT), an examination administered by the

Educational Testing Service to individuals seeking an MBA or other business degree. His request for additional time on the GMAT was subsequently granted.

On April 10, 2006, Jonathan Love submitted a second application for extra time on the September LSAT administration. It contained the original information plus some new reports and records. Whenever an applicant appeals a denial of accommodations, Dr. Dempsey automatically sends the documentation to an outside consultant with expertise in the claimed disability. Dr. Dempsey forwarded Jonathan's documentation to Dr. Charles Golden, a distinguished neuropsychologist currently on the faculty of Nova Southeastern University. Because Dr. Golden concurred with the decision to deny accommodations, Dr. Dempsey sent another e-mail to Jonathan Love that read, "We are not able to grant your request because the documentation provided does not demonstrate that you have a substantial limitation of a major life activity. Therefore, you are not eligible for accommodation under the ADA as a person with a disability."

Undaunted, Mr. Love submitted further documentation: a statement from his mother and a supplemental report from one of his psychologists. Nonetheless, the LSAC again denied his request on June 12, stating, "After consideration of all of the documentation submitted on your behalf, there has been no change in our decision."

Frustrated in his efforts to gain extra time, Mr. Love turned to Disability Rights Advocates, a not-for-profit legal center that takes cases at no charge to its clients. According to their Web site, its mission is "to ensure dignity, equality, and opportunity for people with all types of disabilities in all key areas of life." The description continues: "DRA's national advocacy work includes high-impact class action litigation on behalf of people with all types of disabilities, including mobility, hearing, vision, learning and psychological disabilities. Through negotiation and litigation, DRA has made thousands of facilities throughout the country accessible and has enforced access rights for millions of people with disabilities in many key areas of life, including access to technology, education, employment, transportation and health care."

Through its local attorney, Mr. Weiner, the DRA notified the LSAC on July 13 that legal action would ensue if Jonathan Love did not receive approval of his accommodations request within ten calendar days. The LSAC learned that the formal complaint had been filed on the afternoon of July 31, hours after they had sent the documentation to me for another independent review. According to her testimony at trial, Dr. Dempsey wanted me to evaluate the materials Mr. Love had submitted in anticipation of legal action.

My work with the LSAC began in 1998 when Dr. Dempsey asked if I might join her cadre of outside consultants. At that point I had already provided services to other testing organizations looking for an expert to review documentation; I had also co-edited a book on the topic of accommodations in higher education. I accepted her offer by signing an agreement which established the parameters of my role and an hourly fee.

One motivation for taking on these consultant contracts stemmed from my longstanding research interest in diagnostic procedures, particularly as they relate to the identification of ADHD. I had introduced neuropsychological measures of attention and self-control, written numerous research papers on various aspects of the diagnostic process, and developed a deep interest in identifying factors that distinguish normal from abnormal adjustment. For more than two decades, I have also been director of the ADHD Clinic, one of the longest running such programs in the country. The opportunity to bridge the worlds of clinical practice/research and legal disability determination had always struck me as alluring and important.

The ninety pages of documents that arrived in my in-box contained the following: academic transcripts (10 pages); reports by three different psychologists (43 pages); IOWA Test of Basic Skills profiles (4 pages); score reports forms from SAT, ACT, and GMAT administrations (10 pages); LSAT applicant forms, including two letters of support from staff and faculty at Baylor University (10 pages); a legal declaration by M. Kay Runyan, Ph.D., an expert hired by Mr. Love's attorneys (11 pages); and various correspondences between the LSAC and either Mr. Love or his attorneys (8 pages).

Following well-practiced habits, I reached first for the psychological test reports. The most recent was completed by Hugh J. Van Auken, Ph.D., a clinical psychologist in Indiana. Mr. Love had requested an "assessment compliant with LSAC guidelines" to see if he would qualify for accommodations. The section of the report entitled "Presenting Concern" details the problems Mr. Love and his mother identified at the first appointment:

Attention Deficit/Hyperactivity Disorder. Jonathan indicated that he is diagnosed with an attention deficit/hyperactivity disorder. Jonathan described himself as an inattentive, distractible individual who shows poor concentration. He daydreams excessively and experiences his mind wandering. Jonathan notes that he fails to complete school work in a timely manner, spends excessive amounts of time on homework, and works more slowly than his peers in the graduate school. He indicated that he, "spends two times more time than I should have to" in out-of-class preparation. Ms. Margaret Love, Jonathan's mother, indicated that, "Jonathan has always shown the signs of ADHD." However, she noted that even though symptoms were present throughout childhood, he was not tested for the condition until high school, "because he always received extended time on homework assignments, tests, etc. without having to show record of his impairment." Ms. Love also noted that Jonathan has "always spent a substantial amount of time in completing his work, above average students. He simply works longer to complete assignments to excel in his academics."

Learning Problems. Jonathan reported the presence of ongoing learning problems in reading. He indicated that he demonstrates poor reading comprehension skills, has exceptionally poor reading speed, and forgets much of what he reads. He also reported difficulty completing mathematics tasks in a timely manner. Nevertheless, Jonathan indicated that he currently maintains a 3.2/4.0 grade point average (GPA) in graduate school and received a 3.1/4.0 GPA in undergraduate school.

Social/Behavioral/Psychological Functioning. Jonathan denied the presence of significant ongoing social, behavioral, and psychological problems. He indicated that he is not depressed, overly anxious, or worried.

According to these presenting complaints, Mr. Love would seem to have met at least some criteria for ADHD. He was reported to have experienced a lifelong history of symptoms associated with the disorder (inattention, distractibility, and poor concentration) to a degree that interfered with his ability to handle certain academic tasks. He and his mother also indicated that he had co-existing learning problems, especially "exceptionally poor reading speed," but no other social or psychological difficulties that could account for his reported underfunctioning. Additionally, he was said to have received accommodations via extra time throughout his education.

While the initial section of the report suggested that Mr. Love manifested traits associated with the disorder, it also raised questions about the legitimacy of the ADHD diagnosis for him. The strongest indication that, if Mr. Love suffered from ADHD it would be of the mildest variant, came in the report of his academic performance. When he visited Dr. Van Auken's office, Mr. Love was enrolled in Notre Dame's MBA program with a respectable grade point average of 3.2, a solid record that matched his undergraduate performance. While he reportedly had to work harder than most, he nonetheless was able to handle a prestigious postgraduate curriculum. The question that jumped to my mind upon reading that information was as follows: How impaired is this fellow if he has been able to perform well in a masters-level program, notwithstanding that he had to work hard and may have received some informal accommodations?

The answer to that question, of course, sat at the heart of my documentation review and the legal action that ensued. Is it plausible that someone could suffer from a disorder of attention, concentration, and impulse control, yet still function academically better than most people? Some might respond that, yes, it is absolutely conceivable and, in fact, common that someone with Mr. Love's level of academic attainment had ADHD nonetheless. They would argue that he was only able to excel because of extraordinary compensations, hard work, and the aid of test accommodations. The mere fact that he struggled more than most other graduate students could be construed as evidence that he had an underlying disorder that limited his capacity to achieve his full potential. To be sure, this was the essence of the argument that Mr. Love's clinicians and attorneys made from the outset: If someone of above average abilities struggles (or fails) to accomplish an academic goal, that struggle must reflect the impact of a disorder.

Diagnostic criteria for ADHD and the dictates of the Americans with Disability Act prod a documentation reviewer like me toward other considerations. Unfortunately, explaining those principles will necessarily evoke my baser professorial instincts to lecture. But it is important to understand that a logic underlies the process by which consultants form a disability determination. It is not a voodoo ritual.

Let's start with diagnostic criteria because they form the basis for the first question an LSAC expects me to entertain: Does the documentation provide convincing clinical evidence that Mr. Love suffers from ADHD?

The diagnostic guidelines are set forth in what is known as the "DSM-IV" (the fourth edition of the "Diagnostic and Statistical Manual of Mental Disorders" published by the American Psychiatric Association). The DSM-IV lists diagnostic criteria for all recognized psychiatric disorders, from anxiety and depression to insomnia and anorexia. It represents the gold standard for psychiatric diagnosis, albeit a standard that changes in response to the forces of zeitgeist and clinical research.

The criteria for ADHD begin with a listing of symptoms in two categories: 1) *Inattention*—with items like "is often easily distracted by extraneous stimuli" and "often has difficulty sustaining attention in tasks or play activities"; and 2) *Hyperactivity-Impulsivity*—including items like "often leaves seat in classroom or in other situations in which remaining seated is expected," "often has difficulty awaiting turn," and "often interrupts or intrudes on others." The DSM expects clinicians to diagnose an individual with this disorder if he or she shows six or more symptoms in each list for at least six months and "to a degree that is maladaptive and inconsistent with developmental level." Each symptom must also be present "often" as opposed to occasionally or infrequently.

Many clinical protocols as well as research studies focus on these symptom lists as the Holy Grail of identification. The most common diagnostic tools we clinicians use in our practices are ADHD rating scales based on variants of these items. Typically, the scale will list an item like, "fails to complete assignments," along with response options ranging from "never" to "often." We ask parents, teachers, and the patient to complete such items so we can see the extent to which they identify these symptoms as present. Researchers also rely heavily on symptom rating scales to tag subjects as having ADHD.

While they commonly take center stage in evaluations, symptoms alone do not a diagnosis make. The DSM-IV requires consideration of four other criteria. Criterion "B" indicates that some hyperactive-impulsive or inattention symptoms cause impairment prior to the age of seven. The logic behind establishing an early age of onset is as follows: Extensive research has shown that the ability to pay attention and exert self-control is central to a child's healthy growth and adjustment. In fact, much of what children need to learn, whether at home, in the classroom, or on the playground, hinges on the capacity to stop their behavior long enough to allow for a considered response. Without an adequate ability to inhibit behavior, children will inevitably encounter trouble learning rules, getting along with others, controlling emotions, acquiring academic skills, benefiting from past experience, and anticipating future events. The capacity to exert self-control and concentrate is so necessary for normal development that any deficits in these areas would necessarily have an early and observable impact on adjustment in the same way that a reading disability would be obvious during the years children typically learn to read.

The exact age at which symptoms must be discernable and impairing is hotly debated at the moment. The official criteria listed in the DSM-IV require impairment before age seven years. Indeed, most adults who meet criteria for ADHD manifested problems prior to the school years. However, because at least a quarter of well-defined groups of ADHD adults failed to show problems until the end of the elementary school years, some experts recommend an extension of this criterion to the beginning of puberty (around twelve to fourteen) at the latest. Therefore, while there may be changes in the DSM-IV's requirement for age of onset, it is highly unlikely that the upper limit will extend beyond fourteen years of age.

For individuals who meet criteria for the ADHD diagnosis, amassing such evidence of early impairment is an all-too-easy task. They can provide clinicians with numerous accounts of poor academic performance, impaired social adjustment, and, in many cases, highly impulsive and unruly behavior. Even adults born prior to the advent of special education laws can offer evidence of maladjustment in the form of old report cards, transcripts that show significant academic problems and instances of having failed a grade, teacher narratives that document frequent disruptive behavior, and accounts by parents, relatives, neighbors, and other adults of serious management problems from early in life. These ADHD symptoms emerge despite reasonable efforts at compensation on the part of the child, parents, and teachers.

The next element of the diagnosis, "Criterion C," focuses on establishing that the symptoms disrupt someone's adjustment with relative consistency from setting to setting (namely home, school, and the community). ADHD affects more than just discrete slices of social interaction or job performance. The concept here is that it represents a "hard-wired," enduring set of characteristics that have a broad impact on a person's functioning. Except in unusual circumstances, an individual with ADHD will show those characteristics much of the time and in most situations.

Studies that have followed ADHD children through their lives have amply documented the impact of the disorder on adjustment. In almost all areas of functioning, from academics to occupational performance to marital adjustment to vulnerability to substance abuse, ADHD individuals demonstrate widespread impairment. They are more likely to be fired from jobs, find themselves unemployed, enjoy a lower socioeconomic status than family members, experience more traffic accidents, get their license suspended, acquire a sexually transmitted disease, and have a child out of wedlock. Despite all the claims that ADHD can be an advantage, not one scientific study I am aware of has demonstrated that being abnormally impulsive and distractible is an asset. Anyone who glamorizes this disorder is unfamiliar with the data on the outcome of children who start out life in the ADHD lane.

The DSM-IV's "Criterion D" for ADHD has been the primary target of my scholarly pursuit and research energies over the years. It is the guideline that requires "clear evidence of clinically significant impairment in social, academic, or occupational functioning." The idea here is simple, yet crucial to identifying a psychiatric disorder: diagnoses should only be assigned to individuals whose symptoms cause them to function abnormally in activities that are central to normal adjustment. The reason diagnoses like ADHD stipulate an impairment criterion stems from the reality that a person can have ADHD symptoms without suffering unduly from them. Conversely, an individual might not exhibit that many symptoms, but nonetheless endure a disrupted life.

What constitutes the evidence that being symptomatic is not the same as being disordered? It comes from several sources, chief among them studies that explore the relationship between rating scales that assess symptoms (inattention, for example) and those that look at impairment likely due to those symptoms (perhaps motor vehicle accidents or a poor grade point average). Along with colleagues, I published a paper that calculated the extent of association between these two dimensions in various groups of subjects of different ages and using an assortment of scales. We found a consistent pattern of results, especially with children: while measures of symptoms and impairment are related, the relationship is modest, at best. Our findings suggested that symptoms were a relatively weak predictor of how someone actually functioned.

The partial unlinking of symptoms and the impairment those symptoms cause has weighty implications. For the most part, clinicians have assumed a tight connection between the two domains. Much of the training of mental health professionals, especially those that follow a medical model, is symptom-centric. If you ask a psychiatric resident to list criteria for Major Depressive Disorder, he will catalog the defining symptoms: depressed mood, diminished pleasure, insomnia, loss of energy, and the like. Chances are that he will not take the next step by indicating that those symptoms must be shown to cause the person distress or impairment. The assumption is that a person who tells you he is sad and undermotivated is necessarily maladjusted. Not so, however. Some of us are dour in style, but not especially miserable or unstable.

In the case of ADHD, it is especially important to remember that many of us, especially during the early years, reside on the impulsive, hyperactive, and distractible side of life. We clinicians worry if a child is *overly* serious and constrained. And the mere fact that someone can be inattentive or disorganized is not necessarily reflective of significant impairment. All of us, whether or not we have psychiatric problems, are prone toward a degree of inattention or impulsiveness. The ability to attend and exert self-control is therefore like all other abilities, from running speed to IQ to height to musicality, in that it falls along a normal curve within the general population. Some of us are notable for our attentiveness, others for our inattentiveness, and most of us fall somewhere in the middle.

A psychiatric problem like ADHD represents a normal trait manifested in the extreme. It characterizes people who reside on the far end of the normal curve for a dimension of behavior that is critical to healthy adjustment. As such, the mere fact that an individual is inattentive does not mark him or her as having ADHD.

To be fair, the ADHD diagnosis is not the only one based on cut points along a continuum for a human trait. All psychiatric disorders are defined by drawing lines in the sand. Where's the boundary between being sad and formally depressed? Between being a worrier and meeting criteria for an anxiety disorder? Between being a perfectionist and having obsessive-compulsive personality disorder? Is there really a difference between someone who has a seventy IQ (categorized as Borderline) as opposed to a sixty-nine IQ (categorized as Retarded)? Remember that 13 percent of the U.S. population (roughly 25 million individuals) became non-retarded overnight when, in 1973, the American Association on Mental Deficiency (AAMD) revised the upper boundary for what constituted retardation. The cure for mental retardation required only a pronouncement and a pen.

Diagnosis in physical medicine is similarly based on fungible guidelines. With the exception of pregnancy and certain parasitic infections, medical conditions flow from committee-generated criteria. In July 2004, federal health officials drastically reduced the threshold for what constitutes harmful cholesterol, thereby modifying guidelines they had set only two years prior. Similarly, the National Heart, Lung, and Blood Institute released in 2003 new guidelines for normal blood pressure, lowering the standard from anything less than 140 over 90 to less than 120 over 80. Whether you consider the driving or drinking age, the number of years a politician can serve in office, or how many articles are required for tenure, our world is carved more by arbitrary strokes than laser cuts.

Now we arrive at the question at the core of psychiatric diagnosis: What rules should we use to differentiate between a normal personality style and a mental illness? Put another way, how impaired does someone have to be to qualify as disordered? Here's where the DSM-IV proves least useful. It gives little guidance as to what constitutes "clear evidence" and "clinically significant" impairment. The best hint comes from wording in the symptom list where it indicates that the problem must be "maladaptive and inconsistent with developmental level." But even that phrase leaves ample room for interpretation. Is someone's functioning fairly characterized as "maladaptive" because his distractible style makes him a somewhat inefficient executive? Maladaptive compared to whom? Other executives? People of similar intellectual ability?

Clinicians, if they focus at all on this question of impairment, diverge widely from one another in their decision-making rules. Some will adopt the position that an individual who seeks help for a mental problem must have a problem of some type, simply by dint of the effort. They believe that anyone who is sufficiently distressed to seek services (or to bring a child for services) has difficulties worthy of psychiatric care.

Other practitioners are marginally more conservative in that they will look for evidence of some degree of underperformance that can be tied to the presenting complaints. As an example: Jeremy's parents bring him to an evaluation for ADHD and learning disabilities because, despite his superior IQ, he only has a "B" average in sixth grade. They feel that he could do better were he to be more attentive to his work. Many clinicians would regard that relative discrepancy between his intellectual capacity and actual performance as evidence of impairment. As you will hear, this is the stance Jonathan Love's clinicians adopted in their evaluations. It is also how most school districts identify learning disabled students. Abnormality is judged relative to a person's own array of strengths and weaknesses, not against an external norm.

A somewhat narrower view of disability compares the person's functioning to what is typical of other people, but limits that comparison to birds of similar feathers. In Jeremy's case, the argument would run as follows: "Sure, Jeremy gets average grades but, compared to other people with a high IQ, he is not functioning as well." The logic is most often applied to adults. For example, clinicians will write in documentation that the law student who is applying for accommodations on the bar examination should be judged against other law students, not against the general population. In a way, they argue that you are as disabled as the company you keep. Why, they ask, should a law student be compared to a plumber when it comes to decisions about receiving extra time on a bar examination?

The most restrictive metric for assessing impairment eschews relative discrepancies between aptitudes and abilities as a basis for decision making. Instead, it regards an individual as disordered if, compared to most people in the general population, he shows a significantly diminished capacity to meet age-appropriate expectations in major life activities, such as work, school, social relations, and self-care. In clinical parlance, this model requires that the person show significant deficits in functioning as *compared to the average person*. By this standard, underachieving Jeremy does not have a disorder because he performs at least as well as most children, despite the fact that he could perhaps perform even better. He would only be identified as having a psychiatric or learning problem if, compared to other sixth graders, he was outright abnormal in reading, writing, or math. How abnormal is abnormal? Again, because no bright line of abnormality exists in nature, statistical convention takes over. In this case, the lower 5–10 percent of the normal population often serves as the metric.

Judging impairment by the "average person standard" is anathema to many parents, clinicians, and advocates for the disabled because they regard it as an impediment to people getting help they need to reach their full potential. Jeremy's parents, frustrated because their bright son is getting only Bs, are not terribly interested in the niceties of disabilities determinations or the plight of those with more significant academic failures. They want services that might raise his grades to reflect that high IQ. The clinicians those parents engage to help document a need for services are similarly motivated to help Jeremy fare better. Parents are more likely to be satisfied with professional services (and pay for them) when they lead to the desired outcome. Also, by their nature, clinicians are oriented toward helping those in distress. As a group, they resist limits on their impulse to provide aid to those in need.

The final criterion requires that clinicians rule out all the many other reasons why an individual can be inattentive and impulsive. Because ADHD traits are common to normal people as well as those with various psychiatric and medical problems, professionals regard them as "nonspecific" symptoms. Their presence alone does not define a particular disorder. A symptom like hallucinations is not as common amongst the normal population or people with mental problems. It is more specific to serious mental disorders like schizophrenia or manic depressive illness.

Inattention is an especially woolly symptom because it can emerge as a feature in any number of psychiatric, educational, medical, or routine life circumstances, from schizophrenia, depression, and anxiety to migraine headaches, boredom, and unrecognized cognitive limitations. Inattention as a symptom therefore resembles fever or chest pains in that its presence alone does little to narrow the field of diagnostic possibilities. It simply means that the individual is beset with something of sufficient magnitude to reduce concentration.

To rule out these alternate explanations, the DSM-IV requires a "differential diagnosis" whereby the clinician systematically eliminates other possibilities. We do so by exploring the degree to which the patient reports problems that might meet criteria for other disorders. The strategy most of us take in diagnostic interviews is akin to, "All right, I have a good sense now about the concerns you have related to disorganization and problems concentrating. But I want to make sure we hear about any and all problems you (or, in the case of parents, your child) might have that fall outside of ADHD-type issues. So we're going to run through other problem areas so we don't miss anything." We will now ask about anxiety, depression, mania, obsessive-compulsive tendencies, indications of strange thinking or odd behavior, substance use (sadly, nowadays even for young children), learning disabilities, sleep problems, health complications, enuresis (wetting), encopresis (soiling), relationship troubles, and anything else that might represent a barrier to normal adjustment. We will also inquire about traumatic events that could alter someone's functioning.

Earnest exploration of competing diagnostic possibilities is a clinical journey of utmost value. As I began writing this paragraph, one of the child psychology interns I supervise interrupted, providentially, to tell me about the latest installment in a case that illustrates this point perfectly. Nine-year-old Scott was referred to our child psychiatry clinic because he was inattentive, impulsive, underachieving, and disruptive. While the teachers appreciated his lively imagination and palpable intelligence, they found it hard to manage him in the classroom, as did his classmates when they tried to engage him in play activities. The heavy betting by all involved (including the intern) was that he would soon be visiting the school nurse's office for his morning dose of stimulant medication.

Were it not for a few comments the little boy made to the intern, the road to Ritalin would have been a short one. For example, he told her that he could not always pay attention because he had columns in his head that needed to be counted. Also, embedded in an otherwise normal conversation, were some odd comments about his bathroom habits. These remarks were all unusual enough to reinforce a due diligence consideration of non-ADHD explanations for his classroom troubles.

That search eventually produced irrefutable evidence that Scott's problems with attention were part and parcel of serious emotional disturbance. He divulged that he was inattentive in class because of the armies of clones, arrayed in columns, which were fighting in his head. He was concerned that, if he did not try to manipulate the generals of those armies, terrible things would happen to his family. The more our clinician probed, the more she found psychotic-type thinking and instances of poor reality testing, all of which were starkly confirmed by psychological testing and follow-up interviews with his parents and teachers. While Scott may need medication at some point in his future, it will not be prescribed to treat ADHD.

The benefits of conducting a differential diagnosis extend beyond affirming that ADHD best fits the constellation of problems with inattention and impulsiveness that the person reports. It also ensures that we identify any disorders that might coexist with ADHD. As I wrote in a chapter title for a book on ADHD in adults, ADHD is a disorder that loves company. Between 70 and 80 percent of individuals who meet criteria for ADHD also suffer from at least one other psychiatric or learning disorder. For children, the most common sidekicks are "Oppositional Defiant Disorder" and learning problems. For adults, anxiety, depression, and antisocial behavior are frequent tagalongs. Regardless, the chances are high that we will hear about other difficulties. In fact, it is also the case that we often are confronted with patients who meet criteria for ADHD, but for whom ADHD is the least of their problems. Good treatment planning stems from understanding the totality of a person's circumstance, not just from flagging a single problem domain.

These are the DSM criteria for ADHD that rumbled through my brain as I leafed through those first few pages of Dr. Van Auken's psychological report. While Jonathan and his mother identified symptoms associated with the disorder and reported an early history reflective of some impairment, I tripped on the account of his solid grades in both undergraduate and graduate degree programs. Even if I were to accept that he met criteria for ADHD as a child, it would be hard to establish that these symptoms were limiting his functioning globally now that he was a young adult. Yes, between 50 and 80 percent of individuals identified as having ADHD during childhood will still meet those criteria in adulthood. But not every child with ADHD is destined to a lifetime of ADHD-type impairment.

More importantly, scientific investigations that follow children with ADHD over the life span (these are known as longitudinal studies) have documented how rare it is for them to graduate from college, let alone a postgraduate program. In one of the most rigorous studies conducted by Dr. Russell Barkley, only 5 percent of the original sample of ADHD-identified children graduated from a four-year college. Even now, when most of the participants are in their mid-to-late twenties, not one participant has made it to graduate school. To the best of my knowledge, none of the ADHD children from any of the longitudinal studies has earned a postgraduate degree like an MD or MBA.

The sad reality is that college is an unlikely destination for most children with this disorder. Research has carefully documented the degree to which ADHD limits academic adjustment and attainment. Individuals identified as having ADHD during childhood are more likely than others to be held back at least one grade, placed in special educational services, expelled or suspended because of poor behavior, and drop out of high school altogether. They are also far less likely to enter college than normal children. Academic settings, with all their demands for attention, organization, and impulse control, are the educational equivalents of toxic waste dumps for youngsters who by nature are inattentive, disorganized, and impulsive.

While I may have stumbled on the sentence in Dr. Van Auken's report about Jonathan's enrollment in a prestigious graduate program, I almost fell over when I read this sentence on page 3: "Prior to enrolling at Notre Dame, he received an LSAT score of 150 and a GMAT score of 510 without accommodations." As best I remembered from when my oldest son took the LSAT, a score of 150 was about average. Sure enough, when I looked on the LSAC Web site, the range of scores was between 120 and 180, with 150 hitting just about at the 50th percentile. I remember thinking to myself, "How in the world could this clinician claim that Jonathan Love was disabled when he had already scored in the average range on a high level, professional exam most people aren't even in the position to take?"

The rest of that paragraph did little to diminish my skepticism. It divulged that he scored around the 55th percentile on two administrations of the ACT and roughly the 60th percentile on as many administrations of the SAT. He took all of these examinations under standard conditions. Dr. Van Auken also reported: "Jonathan received no accommodations in high school, middle school, or elementary school. He was never retained at grade level and had no history of involvement in special education programming." This picture of normality was qualified only by two assertions: 1) The clinician indicated that, in high school, Jonathan received tutorial assistance for "seventy or eighty percent of my classes"; and 2) While he did not receive formal accommodations at Baylor University, his alma mater, "a number of professors at Baylor provided an informal accommodation of 'extended time on tests of as much time as I needed' or would allow testing to be completed in faculty offices."

The remainder of Dr. Van Auken's report offered few additional details that would support the notion that Mr. Love was impaired. To the contrary, it mentioned that Jonathan had worked as a summer intern for a congressman as well as in a furniture and art gallery, adding that "he had no difficulties on these jobs attributable to an ADHD process." Alongside a description of healthy adjustment at home and in social circumstances, this employment information would alone rule out a diagnosis of ADHD given the requirement for impairment in more than one setting.

I spent a few more hours reading carefully through all the remaining reports, transcripts, letters, and records. I searched for any information that might deflate the bubble of doubt that grew steadily in my mind that Jonathan Love was so impaired as to warrant the diagnosis of a psychiatric disorder. But the more I read, the more it seemed ludicrous to regard him as anything other than normal.

To mention a few other details from that summer's initial documentation perusal: In addition to ADHD, Dr. Van Auken assigned two other diagnoses: a Reading Disorder and a "Learning Disorder NOS (Academic Fluency Disorder, by history)." He justified the Reading Disorder based on a low score from the Nelson-Denny Reading Test (NDRT), a measure that became the focus of much testimony at trial.

The second label was derived from a 2004 evaluation by AliceAnne Brunn, Ph.D., a psychologist from Waco, Texas. She assigned that diagnosis based on two sets of scores derived from psychological testing. What I found intriguing about the assignment of those additional diagnoses was that Mr. Love did not list them on the "Candidate Form" he submitted to the LSAC when he applied for accommodations in 2006. ADHD was the only disability he identified as warranting the accommodation of extra time. The omission of these other two disabilities was curious. Why not include them if they were legitimate?

Even more peculiar, though, was the "Learning Disorder NOS (Academic Fluency Disorder, by history)" diagnosis that Drs. Brunn and Van Auken assigned. Why? Because there is no such thing as an Academic Fluency Disorder. You won't find it in the DSM- IV or in the scientific literature. It was clinician-manufactured, as best I could tell. My suspicion, later to be confirmed, was that Dr. Brunn took it upon herself to create a new diagnosis as a way of lending weight to her claim that Jonathan needed extra time because he processed academic material slowly. A clinician's credibility plummets in the mind of a documentation reviewer when the zeal to advocate for a client overtakes good judgment and accepted practice.

That Dr. Van Auken carried over a diagnosis from Dr. Brunn who, as it turns out, carried over a diagnosis from the first clinician to work with Jonathan Love, a Micheal Davenport, Ph.D., speaks much about how to construct a diagnostic house of cards. In the context of ADA documentation, many clinicians will accept uncritically whatever diagnoses were previously assigned, perhaps with the idea that the more diagnoses the better. Perhaps some practitioners more generally are loath to second guess another clinician's opinion out of concern that it will irritate that colleague and also confuse the client.

Data in medical records die hard, no matter how inaccurate or misleading they may be. Once fixed on paper or in a digital format, information becomes an enduring feature of a case's mythology. The consequences can be damaging. A local service agency once referred a boy to us who had an assortment of psychiatric and academic problems. Our intake clinician reported that the social service system had trouble placing this youngster in a foster home because he had a history of sex play with animals. When the psychologist who eventually worked with him tried to track down the details of such prior incidents, she learned that no one ever actually witnessed him engaging in inappropriate acts. A foster parent thought that it might have been possible because she walked in once when the child was rubbing the top hindquarter of the family cat. That was it. Somehow the suspicion morphed into fact that, once encoded in a record, became as much a part of this boy's personal history as his birth weight, almost like a reverse form of identity theft or a psychiatric tattoo.

The final piece of documentation I read was an affidavit submitted by M. Kaye Runyan, Ph.D., a well-known figure in special education circles.

What I should have realized was that the submission of her declaration signaled that formal legal action was under way. But I failed to make that connection, mainly because it is not at all uncommon for applications, especially contested ones, to contain legal documents. Because I have testified in court around ADA-type issues, I am probably more likely than some to see files with a threatening letter from an applicant's attorney; it is just that type of letter that will spur a test accommodations administrator to involve an outside consultant like me. I should have stopped to consider that an affidavit was more than the usual attempt at applying legal leverage.

I also have to admit to thinking that the documentation was so weak as to preclude serious legal action. It was hard for me to imagine that a lawyer would pursue a case in earnest of an examinee who already had earned an average score on the very test in question. I had testified in several hearings involving students who, having failed a high-stakes examination (in one instance nine times), sought an accommodated administration. In a few instances, I testified at hearings because the student was worried that he might not perform optimally. But never had a case gone to court when the examinee had already earned a respectable score.

That Dr. Runyan would lend her support to Jonathan Love's cause was not at all astonishing. She has long been associated with the movement to identify, treat, and accommodate the learning challenges of high-functioning students. A special educator by training, she was the Coordinator of Services to Learning Disabled Students at the University of California at Berkeley where, according to her declaration, she "coordinated the evaluation and diagnosis of hundreds of students with learning disabilities, as well as the joint development of accommodation policies with university deans, faculty and staff." Perhaps of most interest to Jonathan Love's lawyers was that Dr. Runyan had been a consultant to several testing organizations with respect to ADA policies and reviews, among them the LSAC. I imagine the DRA was delighted to have Dr. Runyan contribute a declaration that took issue with her former employer.

I met Dr. Runyan when we both attended a meeting hosted by the organization that develops and administers the ACT exam. We were members of a group formed to review the ACT guidelines for ADA documentation. Only minutes elapsed before our philosophical differences collided. Dr. Runyan contended that it was fair to consider someone as learning disabled if, for example, he had a significant discrepancy between his IQ and academic achievement, even if that achievement was no worse than average. To her way of thinking (and that of many, many others), it is perfectly reasonable to consider someone as having a reading disability if, let's say, they had a superior IQ but only average reading skills. She and those of similar mind regard that relative discrepancy between aptitude and performance as evidence of a disorder. By their reckoning, someone with a superior IQ should be superior across the board of academic achievement.

That argument never made sense to me for many reasons, most of which I had written about in academic journals or spoken about in workshops and seminars. In this instance, though, I held off expounding my usual litany of counterarguments and disconfirming studies to ask her about the following scenario: "Kaye, let's say for a minute you were a family practitioner. A patient comes to your office wanting you to verify a physical disability so he can apply for a blue handicapped parking sticker. You ask the fellow, 'Tell me why you think you're disabled?' And he says, 'Well, doctor, I'm a superior athlete by any measure of athletic ability. But my running speed is only average. That discrepancy between my superior athletic ability and my average running speed makes me physically disabled.' Now, Kaye, wouldn't you laugh him out of your office? I think you'd say, 'Give me a break. You're not disabled. You can't get this sticker because your running speed is still average even though it may not stack up against your overall athletic talent.' No? Now explain to me how that situation is any different from the bright student with average reading speed?"

I cannot recall Dr. Runyan's response to my allegory. As best I remember, she argued that an analogy to physical phenomena was unfair because learning was somehow different. But to my mind, it was a perfectly fair comparison. I felt then, as I do now, that it is just as silly to label as learning disabled the bright student whose worst score is still normal as it is to hand out handicapped parking stickers to superior athletes with average running speed.

Mind you, that stance is mighty unpopular in many circles. Many (if not most) of the students identified as learning disabled and ADHD are identified as such based on relative strengths and weaknesses, as opposed to absolute abnormalities. Legions of learning disabled (LD) specialists, tutors, and consultants serve these students, whether they are enrolled in first grade or law school. All universities have an office for disabilities services that provides assistance to, among others, students with these so-called "high-functioning learning disabilities." To people of my conceptual ilk, that designation is oxymoronic. If you are high functioning in a specific domain, you are high functioning. You are not disabled. Disabled is when you are low functioning. Period.

It also has long bothered people like me that a Runyan-type construal of a learning disability or ADHD makes life hard for those who are flat out abnormal in some significant domain. It is far more difficult to get special services for a child with below normal abilities across the board than it is for the "learning disabled" child with a high IQ and a relative weakness. The overall weak learner, because he does not have a discrepancy, is unlikely to come under the auspices of the special education enterprise. Meanwhile, the strong learner with a relative weakness will get the special help and accommodations.

The same circumstance holds for students in postsecondary education. In an article for the *Journal of Learning Disabilities*, my co-authors and I wrote about this problem as follows:

> Consider two students, Joe and Fred, who are both enrolled in a college English course. Joe, who has generally average abilities across the board, would never qualify for an LD label. Fred, on the other hand, was identified as LD because his average scores in reading comprehension compared poorly to his other, more exceptional skills and to his high IQ. Based on this designation, the university granted Fred extra time for examinations. Even though both Joe and Fred are both average in reading comprehension, Fred gets a clear advantage on timed tests simply because he is even better in other academic domains. It would be easy to understand why Joe might feel that he was treated unfairly. From his viewpoint, the playing field was tilted in Fred's favor because professionals and administrators wanted to make sure that the brighter student had the best chance of performing above average. And, because accommodations are often unrestricted, Joe might also be upset to learn that Fred probably gets extra time on all tests, not just those that have a heavy demand for reading comprehension. Why should Fred get extra time even on a calculus test that involved little reading? And, to add the proverbial insult to injury, how fair is it that Fred will likely get extra time on important tests such as the LSAT, GRE, or MCAT, even though Joe would certainly also benefit from such an accommodation?

Dr. Runyan's declaration argued the case not for Fred, but for Joe who, in many ways, resembled Jonathan Love. After reviewing her credentials, she staked her position as follows:

> It is my expert opinion that the documentation provided to the LSAC established strong and compelling evidence of the existence of a disability. Jonathan Love submitted complete clinical evaluations performed by highly credentialed professionals under accepted methods and procedures in the profession. In fact, his application contained extensive documentation showing that his disability had been diagnostically assessed and confirmed on three occasions since 2000, and each clinician properly ruled-out other potential causes of Mr. Love's significant reading difficulties (e.g., lack of good education, emotional problems, English as second language, past medical history, etc.).

Furthermore, each diagnosis of Jonathan Love contained the major indicators of a learning disability and/or ADHD, including: (a) cognitive testing that showed significant discrepancies between relevant processing areas, such as between verbal comprehension and recessing speed, as well as additional diagnostic measures indicating significantly slower reading speed than would be expected given other cognitive measures; (b) reported histories consistent with the onset of the disability at an early age; (c) the use of accommodations in prior educational and testing settings, as well as evidence that those accommodations played an important role in allowing Jonathan Love to demonstrate his knowledge and skills; and (d) clinical observations of Jonathan Love indicating significant restrictions in the manner and condition in which he reads, learns, studies and takes tests in pursuit of his chosen course of study or career.

After elaborating her position in some detail, she concluded:

In sum, Mr. Love's documentation and diagnostic assessments provided the LSAC a complete picture of someone with ADHD and a learning disability that substantially limits his ability to read, process information, learn, study and take tests in pursuit of his chosen course of study or career. It is well demonstrated in the professional literature and research that ADHD and learning disabilities can have a severe impact on the condition, manner or duration by which a person reads (making the activity quite difficult and time consuming) without preventing that person from performing well academically. In fact, for highly intelligent people with ADHD and learning disabilities, such as Mr. Love, it is the accommodations which enable them to show their true gifts and perform up to their potential. In contrast to the LSAC's conclusion, it is my expert opinion that Mr. Love is both disabled and in need of extra time and half as a reasonable accommodation on the LSAT.

These two paragraphs nicely capture the mindset of those who hold the position that a Jonathan Love should be granted accommodations. After endorsing the credibility of the three prior clinicians, Dr. Runyan first accepts as fact claims that Jonathan had significant problems with academic performance from an early age that were only ameliorated by the continuous provision of accommodations like tutoring and extra time. Next, she asserts that the testing these clinicians performed documented weaknesses which would necessarily impact all aspects of learning and test-taking. At the heart of her position lay the contention that ADA-type accommodations were intended to enable very intelligent people "to show their true gifts and perform up to their potential." And therein resides the fundamental question that found its way to Judge Surrick's courtroom: Is the intent of the ADA to guarantee that bright people show their true gifts and full potential?

For the record, the psychological testing that Jonathan Love completed over several administrations did not document that he was "highly intelligent." All of the testing indicated that his IQ fell within an average to high average range. His Full Scale IQ, the most global measure of abilities, came in at a solid 114 (a score of 100 is average).

After assuring myself that I had not missed anything significant, I wrote the following review. It followed my usual format: After listing the diagnostic criteria, I examine the extent to which the documentation offered evidence that those requirements were fulfilled. You might notice that I never actually state that Mr. Love's documentation fails to meet legal standards for disability under the ADA. I try not to put myself in the role of a lawyer or disabilities analyst, per se. My approach is to start with the question, "Does the documentation satisfy clinical criteria?" If, as in this case, the answer is "no," my job is done. If an applicant does not meet the clinical criteria for a disorder, he definitely will not meet the legal standard which, as you will read about later, is more stringent.

Examinee: Jonathan Love

Date of review: 8/1/06

Basis of request for accommodations: ADHD, Learning Disability (my comments pertain to the ADHD component of the application)

Impression: As you know, the diagnosis of ADHD hinges on evidence of clinically significant impairment that has a childhood onset. It must be documented beyond self-report that such symptoms have consistently and pervasively disrupted the individual's functioning. Without compelling evidence of early-appearing and chronic impairment across settings, the diagnosis is regarded as inappropriate. Finally, it must also be demonstrated that the symptoms cannot be better explained by other factors.

According to the documentation, Mr. Love's early history was normal to the extent that he was never retained at grade level, placed in special education programming, referred for psychiatric services, or involved in other circumstances that would reflect significant maladjustment. Nothing whatsoever was provided via report cards, transcripts, or teacher comments to document that he was significantly limited in the ability to handle normal developmental, academic, or social tasks. As best one can tell, the examinee was a competent, well-functioning primary school student who, at most, required some informal tutoring. Therefore, the diagnostic criterion for early impairment due to ADHD-type symptoms was not met.

The picture of normal development persists through high school and beyond. For example, standardized achievement testing from 6th-8th grades put him solidly in the average range across the board. Despite his mother's report that his IOWA scores in were "below average and especially low in reading comprehension," his composite and reading total scores were actually around the 80th percentile. He graduated from high school with a 3.24 GPA and without the need for any formal accommodations. His academic record was sufficient to allow admission to Baylor University, from which he graduated with a 3.2 GPA, once again without requiring any formal accommodations.

Most relevant to the current determination stands Mr. Love's record of taking high stakes, timed tests. Without exception, he has scored within an average range under standard conditions for all such examinations, including the SAT, ACT, GMAT, and (most notably) the LSAT. Indeed, his score in the 46th percentile on your test is solidly average. He therefore clearly and demonstrably has the neuropsychological capacity to take a timed examination at least as well as most people. Assertions that he is somehow disabled by ADHD symptoms are based more on the notion that he might do even better were he to receive extended time rather than on credible evidence of actual impairment in test-taking. In my opinion, interpretations of relative discrepancies in psychological test scores pale in significance when compared to ample real-life verification that he is able to take a test as well as most people. The documentation provides evidence that extended time might well not benefit Mr. Love. For example, on the reading comprehension score of the Nelson-Denny Reading Test, he achieved the same standard score for both the regular and extended time administrations (his grade equivalent for the total score was actually lower when he was given more time).

As for more current impairment, the current documentation contains no evidence of global limitations because of ADHD-type symptoms. Nothing was provided via transcripts, faculty comments, job performance reviews, or other sources of information that Mr. Love has shown pervasive problems managing daily demands for organization and attention. To the contrary, it appears that he has functioned well at school, on the job, and in social circumstances.

Because this documentation fails to offer any compelling evidence of either early or current impairment associated with ADHD, I recommend that the request for accommodations be denied.

After pressing the "Send" button on my e-mail, I distinctly remember thinking to myself, "Well, that's the last I'll hear of Jonathan Love. It's a no-brainer. What judge is going to waste his time on this case?" Little did I know.

CHAPTER 2
Motivations

If you were to review my voting record, annual charitable contributions, and professional activities, you would not peg me as a likely invitee to Rush Limbaugh's holiday party. When the government errs, I prefer those mistakes to stem from buying too much butter rather than too many guns. In my view, a society's decency and value is reflected in how it treats the most vulnerable citizens, not the most able and affluent. Social justice and equal opportunity are buzzwords that sound pleasant to my ears. While by no means a bleeding heart, my political impulses lean more toward supporting the individual than the corporate. I am a middle-of-the-road kind of guy with a slight tilt toward the left-hand lane.

So, you might ask, "What in the world were you thinking when you agreed to support a multimillion-dollar corporation engaged in a legal battle with a lowly graduate student who just wanted a few extra minutes on a test?" If you really wanted to cut to the quick, you could say, "Nice. Here you are, a recognized advocate for the mentally ill, throwing your lot in with the bad guys. What's next? Ralph Nader helping GM increase greenhouse gas emissions?"

The accurate, albeit somewhat disingenuous, response: I testified because I reviewed documentation for a testing organization that Jonathan Love took to court. It was not as if I were a hired gun of an expert witness seeking opportunities to testify. In all but one instance, my participation has been driven by subpoena and legal complaint, not financial interest or the love of witness stands. I was involved because I had recommended denial of accommodations to someone who found the wherewithal to sue. And I was never hired by LSAC to deny applicants accommodations. My job was to render an opinion; I was paid the same for that opinion whether my thumb went up or down on the granting of the request. Rather than helping Goliath squash David by looking for ways to withhold accommodations, I was instead involved because David was taking Goliath to court for being unhelpful.

The technical response I just offered would justify why I would write a declaration and serve as an expert witness during the proceedings. I was mandated by the nature of the litigation (unless I wanted to change my opinion altogether). What it fails to explain is why, in short order, I became so deeply invested in *Love* v. *LSAC*. My in-box for the months of August to December contains over 800 e-mail interchanges with the attorneys, at least a third of which I wrote. I spent hours searching the literature on one topic or another, reading depositions, writing out questions the lawyers might ask the plaintiff's experts, and preparing summaries on topics such as the ability of IQ to predict test performance or the validity of the Nelson-Denny Reading Test. As the case progressed, my personal investment of time and mental energy far outstripped the consequences of personal advancement or financial gain (much less critical now as I float gleefully in a euphoric state of post-tuition bliss).

Of the many motivations that fueled my headlong dash into this legal fray, none outmatched the sheer force of righteous indignation. However, not much of it was directed toward Jonathan Love, himself. He is not the first student who has tried to gain advantage over the competition or make up for real or imagined imperfections in motivation or talent. Educators like me are familiar with those outcroppings of entitlement. We have become accustomed to college students demanding that we change the grade from a C to a B because "I need a B average so I don't lose my scholarship," or "My father said he won't pay for my car if my grades are low," or "My parents are spending a huge amount of money for college and don't expect professors to give me low grades." While Jonathan Love may have been a bit cheekier than most when he took his case for special consideration all the way to federal court, a sense of entitlement is by no means unique to him.

The blame can be cast widely for what might be a national case of over-entitlement amongst students. For every Jonathan Love, you will find at least one teacher, clinician, or administrator who, somewhere along the way, should have stood up to the quest for special privilege with a firm "no way." In Jonathan's case, the list of those who enabled his pursuit of legal accommodations is lengthy. Any one of three clinicians could have told him years earlier, "Listen, Jonathan, I'm really sorry but it makes no sense to construe your perceived underachievement as related to ADHD or a learning disability. It's not fair to you and it's not fair to others. You might not be perfect, but you sure aren't substantially impaired. How about we talk about other avenues you could pursue, like a speed reading course or help for test anxiety? Those kinds of interventions would likely improve your scores not only on the LSAT, but on other tests as well." Instead, the clinicians jumped on the ADHD bandwagon, fully supporting Love's sense that he somehow deserved unique consideration.

Gatekeepers were off duty elsewhere, too. The GMAT granted him extra time on the graduate school entrance examination. Because they saw much of the same material Jonathan Love submitted to the LSAC, their rationale for considering him as disabled is murky. However, all academic institutions and test organizations are free to set their own standards for what they consider to be a disability. While the law sets the highest point the bar can be set, it does not preclude lower positions. The problem, of course, is that those looser standards set a precedent that can make a more rigorous position harder to maintain.

Because Jonathan Love did not request accommodations from Notre Dame or Baylor University (a fact the defense later used to bolster the contention that he was not disabled), these universities did not have to decide whether to identify him as an individual covered by the Americans with Disabilities Act. If they responded like most institutions, however, they would have granted the request. Because academic institutions have little incentive to deny accommodations, most students who apply for them will receive those benefits without hesitation. Educational organizations can benefit from granting accommodations because it helps them meet many of their primary goals: keeping students in school, getting good grades, earning high scores on admissions tests, and gaining acceptance to postgraduate training.

Now that the *US News & World Report* rankings have become the performance benchmark for higher education, academe has become preoccupied with meeting those magazine-generated standards. Freshman retention rates, graduation rates, and the percent of students who ascend to postgraduate training are all elements of those rankings. If a student might get a higher LSAT score with extended time, the impulse will be to support that cause because that higher score will help to make the institution shine. If a college can increase the chances of a weak student staying in school by affording him more time on tests, a notetaker, and tutorial services, that can be good for the rankings.

You can be sure that the *US News & World Report* protocol avoids tracking an educational institution's efforts to afford accommodations only to those who, according to the law, are truly disabled. Colleges and universities derive little benefit from withholding disability services and test accommodations from those non-disabled students who simply want a higher grade point average or a better score on high-stakes tests like the LSAT. Denial of disability status only exposes them to lower rankings, disgruntled students, fuming parents, loss of tuition, and legal challenges.

Academic deans are among those most tightly pressed between maintaining standards and respecting disability rights. Imagine you were a Dean of Students at a major university. You are sitting with Robert, a freshman, because he is failing all but two courses after having barely survived his first semester. You have talked to several of the faculty, all of whom have the feeling that Robert tries hard but is not especially adept at managing post-secondary level coursework, in part because his high school may not have prepared him well enough. Also, he did not strike anyone as having the attitude or aptitude to make the most of a four-year program. The consensus of opinion was that it would be best for him to seek an educational program that better suited his matrix of abilities. Because he impressed one of the professors with his graphic design skills, the idea arose that Robert might apply to a program that would maximize those talents.

Two choices lie before you. One is to say, "I am really sorry, Robert, but it doesn't look like a challenging university program of the sort we offer is a good match for you. When we selected you, we truly thought you would thrive in our university but, unfortunately, it hasn't worked out that way. Our sense is that you would do much better for yourself in another setting, perhaps one geared more to your specific interests and abilities. Rather than continuing to struggle in this program, wouldn't it be better for you to make other plans?"

Your other tack is to construe Robert's academic hardships as the reflection of a disability. You could say to him, "Robert, we have to figure out why you are having such a hard time in your classes. Because we selected you with the expectation that you would excel, it must be that you have some learning disability or attention problem that is lowering your grades. We're going to refer you to our psychology clinic so they can identify the nature of that disability. And then we'll make sure you get extra time on tests and also help from the disability services. Yes, I know that you've never been identified with a problem earlier in your life and that you did well in high school. But maybe you were able to compensate before the material became more difficult."

Which option represents the path of least resistance? The disability route, without a doubt.

To be fair, each option has its share of upsides and downsides. Option #1 has the advantage of being more immediately productive in that Robert would be forced to rethink his educational goals and plan accordingly.

Without too much delay, he might enroll in that graphics design program at a local technical college en route to a career in the field. The shortcoming, I suppose, comes from the tiny but real possibility that he had a true disability that was somehow masked over the years by extraordinary efforts at compensation. Also, even if he were not formally disabled, he might have benefited from accommodations enough that he might have been able to graduate with a four-year degree. The potential benefit of Option #2, then, is that Robert might land a better job than he might otherwise, a job that he could manage either with similar accommodations or without any at all.

The disability route also has associated risks. What if Robert is granted the accommodations but still fails too many courses to graduate or he graduates with a grade point average so low that his employment options become limited? Where is Robert now other than out considerable sums in tuition payments and years behind in his quest to head down a suitable career path? And what if he gets that better job, yet finds it such a struggle that he performs marginally even with accommodations? He might end up over-accommodated but under-employable.

We can also play the Robert scenario out further to illustrate how entitlements and expectations can cascade. Robert now comes back from the psychologists with the diagnosis of a learning disability based on some relative weaknesses on selected scores from psychological testing. He becomes entitled to extra time, adjustments in his course load, test accommodations, and individual tutoring. Some of his professors also extend deadlines for the completion of certain labs and projects. With these adjustments in his academic program, Robert manages a C average through his junior year.

Somewhere in the fall of his senior year, Roger decides that he would like to become a lawyer like his father. Having received accommodations during college, he assumes he is entitled to them on the LSAT. He downloads the application, sends the documentation to the LSAC, and waits for confirmation that his request for double time was approved. He is shocked to learn that his application was denied because, in the LSAC's judgment, the documentation failed to support a diagnosis of a learning disorder or a legal qualification of disability. What happened?

The problem for Robert is that the rung on the educational ladder he would like to climb has become harder to grab because the ground below has begun to shift. Whereas his college was motivated to keep him progressing through their program, the LSAC is more keyed on the viability of their test. Specifically, they must warrant that the LSAT represents a reasonably accurate predictor of how a student will perform in law school. If those admissions officers lose faith in the test's capacity to predict performance (like some of their college counterparts have for the SAT and ACT test scores), the LSAC is out of business. Consequently, they worry at least as much about the sanctity of their testing procedures as Robert's accommodations request.

Should LSAC worry that willy-nilly approval of extra time could affect the test's ability to predict outcome? According to research, the answer is "yes." The data show that the test's ability to predict law school performance is undermined if time parameters are extended. Scores derived from extended-time administrations over-predict law school grade point averages (for example, high scores are less likely to foretell high grades). Those data are presented at http://members.lsacnet.org/ in the "Research" section. You will find a research report entitled, "Speed as a Variable on the LSAT and Law School Exams" by William D. Henderson. If you scroll down to the "Technical Reports" you will encounter another relevant article, "Predictive Validity of Accommodated LSAT Scores" by Andrea E. Thornton, Lynda M. Reese, Peter J. Pashley, and Susan Dalessandro.

Both studies provide convincing evidence that the LSAT is, in part, what is known as a "speeded" test. The accuracy of its predictions is aided by how quickly the student is able to complete the exam. Of course, it also has a substantial "power" component in that students must also have what it takes at any speed to read well and solve items involving verbal reasoning. But the pace at which the examinee manages those tasks is relevant. The same conclusions can be drawn, incidentally, for the SAT. Extending the time diminishes the test's validity as it relates to predicting freshman year performance.

To complete the Robert scenario: Imagine now that, for whatever reason, Robert was granted accommodations on the LSAT and that he earned a score sufficient to allow him admission to a law school. With the help of further accommodations and an extra year of study, he receives his law degree. Passing the bar stands as the last hurdle to gainful employment as a lawyer. Inevitably, Robert files his application for accommodations on the bar examination with the state board of law examiners.

Now the vector of incentives changes dramatically. The board of bar examiners has as its primary responsibility the protection of public safety and trust. It must ensure to the extent possible that individuals who are allowed to practice law in that state have the requisite knowledge and skills. Notwithstanding the stereotypes broadcast by all those lawyer jokes, the board also has to certify that the applicant has "character and fitness."

Bar examiners are the final gatekeepers on the road to an individual becoming a lawyer because, once admitted to the bar, a lawyer is free to hang up a shingle and keep it dangling for the duration. The consequences of a poor decision can be substantial, especially for a profession that can literally become involved in matters of life and death, freedom or incarceration, affluence or poverty. It is easy to understand why these bar examiners might err on the side of stringency.

Bar examiners are only one group of many charged with maintaining standards of practice. Name the profession and you will find at least one credentialing organization with the weighty responsibility of protecting the public from unqualified doctors, dentists, accountants, veterinarians, engineers, architects, pilots, financial planners, and so forth. The stakes are perhaps highest for medical licensing boards. They must ensure that the doctors who treat us have demonstrated a modicum of competence in all aspects of medicine. The medical boards rely to a large extent on a medical student's performance on a series of evaluations called the "Step" exams, administered by the National Board of Medical Examiners (NBME). These carefully crafted tests measure a medical student's knowledge of basic medicine, clinical knowledge and skills, and specialty competence. You can be sure that the NBME is intent on maintaining rigor in the process.

Jonathan Love, like Robert, found it hard to understand why he could not have extra time to earn an LSAT score he felt reflected his intelligence and hard work. At trial he said that he sought legal counsel because he saw no other way to earn the accommodations he felt were required if he were to gain admissions to a top tier law school. Overly-entitled? Perhaps. But his outsized expectations were small change in the panoply of reasons I became so involved in this case. I will not generally become too exercised when humans act like humans. A little annoyed, sometimes, but usually not enough to grab a placard or spend most free moments mulling over legal arguments and strategies.

That same attitude applied to Jonathan's mother, Margaret Love, a central figure in this story. She provided two of the clinicians with critical information about Jonathan's childhood functioning. She also testified at the trial. While her fealty to the truth may have been somewhat more fragile than most, it was hard for me to aim too much antipathy her way. Most parents will do about anything to help their children succeed, even if lines are crossed that should be honored.

As for the lawyers, well, it is never a challenge to take offense at the antics of opposing counsel. They have been known to try their level best to discredit you at every turn. But that is what litigators are paid to do. The only thing that bothered me from the outset (as it did all the more during the trial) was what seemed like an unfortunate misallocation of resources. Rather than helping those who really needed legal expertise, these lawyers were devoting hours of their time to helping a Notre Dame MBA get an even higher score on the LSAT. When I thought of all the patients in our clinic alone who could sorely use legal assistance to take on recalcitrant insurance companies, school systems, and employers, *Love* v. *LSAC* seemed like a terrible waste of talent. Many times I wanted to reach across, grab them by the collar, and shout, "You want to defend disabled people? I'll show you some undeniably disabled people who badly need your help." Although I resisted the urge, the sentiment remained.

Those cases of the legally unrepresented exist by the score. An example: We have an adolescent patient I'll call Monica in our clinic for whom the evidence of bipolar disorder is overwhelming and credible (unlike so many purported cases of bipolar illness in children). She cuts herself when she becomes depressed, routinely falls into a psychotic state, and makes a host of bad choices when her mood swings toward the wrong phase. Although these symptoms have been ongoing for some time, she entered formal treatment only about a year ago.

The problem is that Monica's insurance company only pays for twenty outpatient visits, far fewer than required for someone with a psychiatric disorder as chronic and impairing as hers. Because that allotted quota is now spent, Monica's family has to look for other funding or free services; neither option is easily attained. Monica could use a DRA-type lawyer in her court. Discrimination against individuals with mental illness is rampant and institutionalized. Could you imagine a cardiologist having to tell a heart attack victim, "Sorry, but I have to stop treating your heart condition because the insurance company only pays for five visits?" This scenario would never happen because insurance companies will not cap treatment for a physical problem. That is not the case for psychiatric conditions, even though some can be equally life threatening.

One more example: We have a twelve-year-old boy in our clinic whose school refuses to provide him even minor accommodations. He has an IQ in the borderline range, well-documented problems paying attention and exerting self-control, and a history of learning best in a one-to-one or small group setting. While still of sunny disposition, his frustration with school is beginning to mount as are his doubts about himself as someone who can learn. Relatively inexpensive special educational services, like access to more individualized instruction in a "resource room," would go a long way toward helping him stay in school and make progress. Given this district's record of denying services, however, our patient will only get what he needs if his parents have the means to bring legal leverage to bear. But their resources are far too limited to fund action against the school.

So what did kick my involvement in the Love case into high gear? No small portion of the mix was outrage at my own colleagues in the mental health professions. Far too often, the evaluations they submit on their clients' behalf stray far beyond the pale of good practice and reasoned analysis. They reflect a profound lack of knowledge about the Americans with Disabilities Act alongside what I have come to think of as the "Curse of the Desired Outcome." In my opinion, it is the latter phenomenon that most taints the process. It generates the smoke that clouds the judgment of otherwise well-intentioned and competent professionals.

The Curse reflects the consequences of approaching an evaluation dead set on identifying a disability at all costs. Because your agenda is to help your client achieve the desired outcome of test accommodations, you scan the clinical landscape for anything that will help you make that case. You will also minimize the import of any contradictory information because, again, you see your job as advocating for the diagnosis as a way of helping your patient succeed in his or her quest. You decidedly eschew the more dispassionate stance of someone who considers all information objectively before arriving at a decision based on the evidence, not the client's wishes. To one afflicted by the curse, the only data worth considering are those that promote the cause.

Signs that the Curse of the Desired Outcome may have struck a clinician come into view early in reports. Presented below is the introduction to an evaluation I reviewed last week regarding a student looking for extra time on a high-stakes examination. The psychologist who submitted the report (which I have sanitized) states her agenda up front and without remorse:

> Ms. Lisa Seymour is a 28-year-old female who was seen at this office for a comprehensive evaluation of her psychological and educational functioning in order to document her clear need for test accommodations. Ms. Seymour will submit the present report to verify the manifestations of her attention and learning disorder symptoms in terms of functional impairment . . .

So much for an objective evaluation of Ms. Seymour's psychiatric status. Instead, the clinician positions herself immediately as an advocate for assignment of the diagnosis.

Other classic signs of the Curse surface as this report unfolds. The most prominent is what I call "Sour Cherry Picking," the practice of construing every minor perturbation in functioning as necessarily reflecting major abnormality, often by taking selected comments out of context. An example: The clinician makes much of a statement the applicant's fourth-grade teacher recorded on a report card. She said that the student needed a seat belt because she was so energetic. Alongside that remark were the applicant's verbal reports of poor grades and overall underachievement during elementary school. The psychologist jumped on those accounts to justify the conclusion that her client showed clear impairment during the early years earning grades that reflected "academic disappointment and failure." Throughout all the ensuing reports and applications, it became an accepted fact that Lisa Seymour struggled substantially during primary school.

With submission of additional documentation, a more accurate picture emerged. What the clinician failed to mention was that Ms. Seymour was an "A" student who earned academic honors during elementary school. The clinician also mischaracterizes that fourth-grade teacher's comment on the report card. While the teacher wrote that "Lisa needs a seat belt!" she qualified it by adding "at times" and gave her As in all subjects. That teacher further commented on her superb work ethic and level of academic accomplishment, sentiments echoed by teachers in the other grades. Lisa was anything but a survivor of "academic disappointment and failure" during elementary school. She was a well-adjusted, successful, albeit lively student.

The biased construal of Ms. Seymour's personal history persists throughout the report. The picture of a successful life was recast as a panorama of disability, with each feature regarded as a testament to ADHD-induced hardship. Another example: The examinee earned an LSAT score in the 80th percentile. One might think a score at that level might reflect some degree of competence given the test's complexity and the intense competition for high scores. But, no, this clinician regards that score as proof of disability when she writes: "Ms. Seymour *only* [my italics] scored in the 80th percentile, well below her potential and therefore reflective of her ADHD." In the eyes of a clinician hell-bent on identifying a disability, even solid accomplishments can morph into reflections of malady.

The Curse of the Desired Outcome has many other symptoms, most of which surface in the psychological testing reports that Mr. Love submitted for accommodations. You will read much about them in following chapters. But those manifestations of the curse are widespread and rooted in an ill-advised sense of advocacy. I find them counterproductive. Why? Because evaluations for psychiatric disorders, like judgments about other issues in this world, are best made with an open mind, not through the lens of a clinical or ideological agenda. Troubles brew when decision makers pick and choose their facts to justify a predetermined conclusion. In the case of psychiatry, ignoring uncomfortable realities can lead to misdiagnosis, inappropriate treatment, poor allocation of resources, and injustice. To see fellow professionals act so cavalierly with such regularity irritates me no end.

The major propulsion for my involvement in *Love* v. *LSAC*, however, was not fueled by colleague-directed pique. I may be arrogant and pigheaded, but not to such an extent that I'm unable to restrain myself in the face of divergent views. No, what motivated my involvement was a sincere concern about individuals with disabilities. That's right. From the beginning, I saw this case as an offense to those with legitimate limitations. The lawyers I worked with held the same position. The lead attorney for the LSAC's case, Ms. Jane Leopold-Leventhal, said just that when she was interviewed by *The Legal Intelligencer*: "All along, we felt that we were the ones representing the rights of the disabled." She went on to articulate the notion that the rights of the disabled are infringed upon when the non-disabled use disability rights laws to gain advantage.

In my view, *Love* v. *LSAC* was an egregious instance of misguided advocacy, of chutzpah gone wild. By campaigning for the high-functioning, Jonathan Love's advocates undermined the rights and entitlements of those with bona fide handicapping conditions. If Jonathan Love is disabled, almost everyone is disabled because humans, by nature, are flawed. We all have areas of relative weakness that can make us less successful than we might prefer. But if everyone is disabled, no one is disabled. We devolve into a global agglomeration of the imperfect.

The problem, however, is that some people really have substantial challenges in their capacity to handle major life activities like walking, talking, learning, and attending. Their problems in these domains limit their ability to adjust as others can. They deserve protection from discrimination in the workplace, when they take examinations, and during the course of their daily lives.

Their chances of getting that help diminish as skepticism grows about the legitimacy of accommodations for those with mental health disorders. If the general public comes to regard ADHD or LD as just a cheap excuse that successful people use to become more successful, those with substantial difficulties will struggle all the more. They will encounter cynical employers who, when approached by someone looking for ADA protections, might think, "Here we go again. I've gotta deal with someone else looking for a pass because of some boutique disorder." Or a law student who deserves extra time on the bar exam will encounter a suspicious administrator who has seen entirely too many competent people portrayed as impaired. Trivializing what it means to have a disability is no boon to the disabled.

Several years ago I was chatting with a university student who had joined us for a holiday dinner. Along the way she asked me about my work at the medical center. When I told her that much of my research involved ADHD, she responded, "Oh yeah, I know all about sham ADHD. Most of my friends have it." I was taken aback. "Sham ADHD is a common disorder at your university?" She proceeded to tell me that it was common practice for students to claim they had ADHD or a learning disability to gain extra time on exams or a prescription for a psychostimulant. Everyone apparently knew the counselors at the student health center to contact for an evaluation. I thought to myself, "That's just great. Here we've spent years trying to get people to take ADHD seriously only to have it used as a way to score performance enhancing drugs and better grades."

My involvement with this case was therefore not borne of a desire to grind philosophical axes or hostility to the Americans with Disabilities Act. ADHD is a legitimate disorder and the ADA is a great law. My rationale for casting my lot with the LSAC was founded upon concern that a legitimate disorder and a great law were threatened by proceedings that could cause harm to the cause of disability rights.

With that motivation in mind, I was willing take the plunge. And the ensuing preparation for trial quickly provided many opportunities for diving into deep waters.

CHAPTER 3

Diagnosis versus Disability

The case of *Love* v. *LSAC* almost never made it to trial. The complaint was first filed as a request for a preliminary injunction. Mr. Weiner and the DRA wanted the judge to rule just on the pleadings, i.e., the information contained in the legal papers that they and the LSAC submitted to him. They hoped that Judge Surrick would find the DRA arguments so persuasive that he would order the LSAC to grant accommodations without further legal ado. If the judge had ruled in their favor, the LSAC would not have been able to pursue expert depositions, let alone academic records, clinical reports, and other information about the life of Jonathan Love.

In a series of phone calls that took place during the first ten days of August, the lawyers for each side pursued their individual agenda. While the DRA wanted the judge to see no more than the legal filings within the context of a brief hearing, the LSAC pushed for a full trial. They surely wanted the opportunity to gather paper records and depose anyone who might provide relevant testimony. I imagine that, from their standpoint, the judge would need a full airing of the facts if he were to arrive at a fair decision. They also must have had a sense that the information contained in the materials Mr. Love submitted in his quest for accommodations would likely be open to interpretation.

In an August 10, phone conference, Judge Surrick pushed back on the DRA's request for a hearing without witnesses or records. He indicated that, for a hearing to be granted, the plaintiff would have to prove a high likelihood of success on the merits of the case. Further, both sides would have to agree generally on the facts of the case. Because neither condition prevailed, he ordered limited discovery on an expedited basis. He circumscribed depositions to seven expert witnesses: four for the plaintiffs (Drs. Brunn, Van Auken, Davenport, and Runyan), three for the defendants (Drs. Dempsey, Golden, and Gordon). He ordered that these depositions be completed within 30 days, a tiny window for a case in federal court involving experts from across the country. In some complex trials, the discovery phase can actually take years, although my understanding is that most last about 60–90 days.

The judge ordered that this limited discovery transpire swiftly so that a trial could be held as early as October. He quickened the pace because Mr. Love wanted accommodated test scores included in his applications to law school. His lawyers claimed that he would suffer irreparable harm if Jonathan were unable to take the LSAT at the February administration time. According to them, a delay would interfere with his ability to submit his law school applications. Ironically, during arguments around this issue, Ms. Joan VanTol, corporate counsel for the LSAC, revealed to the judge a fact that was also new to the DRA's lead attorney, Mr. Sid Wolinsky. She had determined from the LSAC database that Mr. Love had already been admitted to four law schools based on his academic record and the LSAT score he earned on a standard administration of the test in 2003. That Mr. Wolinsky was unaware of these acceptances did not bode well for the plaintiff's case.

To this day, it mystifies me that Judge Surrick chose not halt the legal proceedings immediately upon hearing that Mr. Love had already been admitted to four law schools approved by the American Bar Association. How could he even consider that Jonathan was disabled? Not only did this MBA student earn an average score on an unusually challenging professional examination, he had amassed an academic record fine enough to allow admission to law school. Remember, only the academic elite even have the option of entering law school. Is it at all possible that Congress intended the Americans with Disability Act (ADA) to protect the rights of a Jonathan Love?

Congress passed the ADA (Public Law 101-336) to prohibit discrimination and ensure equal opportunity for persons with disabilities. The intent of the law was articulated succinctly by President George Herbert Walker Bush at the 1990 signing ceremony:

> This act is powerful in its simplicity. It will ensure that people with disabilities are given the basic guarantees for which they have worked so long and so hard: independence, freedom of choice, control of their lives, the opportunity

to blend fully and equally into the rich mosaic of the American mainstream. Legally, it will provide our disabled community with a powerful expansion of protections and then basic civil rights. It will guarantee fair and just access to the fruits of American life which we all must be able to enjoy. And then, specifically, first the ADA ensures that employers covered by the act cannot discriminate against qualified individuals with disabilities. Second, the ADA ensures access to public accommodations such as restaurants, hotels, shopping centers, and offices. And third, the ADA ensures expanded access to transportation services. And fourth, the ADA ensures equivalent telephone services for people with speech or hearing impediments.

The law embodies President Bush's expressed aims in five sections, of which the first three most impact daily life. Title I requires employers to provide qualified individuals with disabilities an equal chance to benefit from work-related opportunities in hiring, salary, promotion, training, or other "privileges of employment." It not only outlaws discrimination against those with disabilities, but also requires that employers make reasonable accommodations so that someone with a disability can perform his job. Like other anti-discrimination laws such as the Civil Rights Act of 1964 and the Rehabilitation Act of 1973, the ADA seeks to ensure that an individual otherwise qualified for a job has an equal opportunity to compete for and, if hired, work as others do in that position. For example, if a person in a wheelchair were able to perform all the functions of a tax accountant but for narrow office doorways, the ADA would require the firm to disregard the disability in its hiring decisions and to pursue reasonable changes in the office so the person could work there.

Title II covers public transportation services, such as city buses and public rail transit. It requires public transportation authorities to ensure that individuals with disabilities have comparable access to the transit system. It is this section of the ADA that accounts for wheelchair lifts in buses, elevators in airports, and other accommodations on trains, planes, automobiles, and buses that allow everyone to use the system whether or not they are disabled.

The section that has literally changed the face of the country is Title III. It requires anyone who owns or operates a facility that is open to the public (designated under the law as a "public accommodation") to remove any and all barriers that hinder use or participation by someone with a disability. As proclaimed by the General Rule for this section: "No individual shall be discriminated against on the basis of disability in the full and equal enjoyment of the goods, services, facilities, privileges, advantages, or accommodations of any place of public accommodation by any person who owns, leases (or leases to), or operates a place of public accommodation." To ensure a law with societal sweep, the ADA provides categories and examples of what it considers to be a "public accommodation." With few exceptions (mainly related to size), every business and public gathering spot in the nation is covered, from hotels, motels and restaurants, to concert halls, grocery stores, professional offices, and even funeral parlors.

Title III of the ADA is single-handedly responsible for the country-wide changes in road construction, architectural design, and the provision of services. The wheelchair cuts in sidewalks, handicap-accessible bathrooms, wide doors that open automatically when the blue square is pressed, wheelchair ramps, Braille signs on elevator buttons, handicap parking spaces, wheelchair seating in public venues like auditoriums and stadiums, and sign language interpreters at presentations are all the consequence of the ADA's Title III. Indeed, most of us know this legislation primarily as the impetus for the ubiquitous blue handicap symbols that dot the landscape.

Embedded in the language of Title III is one sentence that forms the basis for a Jonathan Love to bring suit against a testing organization like the LSAC. Section 309 reads: "Courses and examinations related to professional, educational, or trade-related applications, licensing, certifications, or credentialing must be provided in a place and manner accessible to people with disabilities, or alternative accessible arrangements must be offered." That sentence has been interpreted as requiring testing organizations to accommodate not only individuals with physical disabilities, but also those with learning, attentional, and psychiatric disorders. Those thirty-four words out of the over twenty-three thousand in the legislation have been the impetus for every college, university, and testing organization in the nation to develop the administrative and service apparatus required to be compliant with the ADA.

Any law, no matter how well intended and carefully crafted, is wide open for interpretation and the emergence of unintended consequences. The Americans with Disabilities Act is no exception, to say the least. Some would offer it as a textbook example of how definitional ambiguities, even in a law most consider of noble intent, can keep regulatory agencies, courts, and attorneys busy for years on end. Consider that litigation around issues inherent in *Love* v. *LSAC* has been ongoing for almost two decades, even though the issues under review still focus on the law's fundamental assumptions and requirements. Beyond all the legal protections the ADA has afforded individuals with disabilities, it has also kept many an attorney, judge, and consultant busy.

The element of the ADA that has most occupied the courts is also the most fundamental: "What qualifies someone as disabled?" The law itself offers only the broadest of definitions. It specifies that an individual can be considered to have a disability if he or she has a physical or mental impairment that "substantially limits one or more major life activities." Those eight quoted words represent the sum total of what Congress offered by way of a definition. The absence of any further clarification has allowed ambiguity and interpretation to run amok.

Nothing in the act helps to clarify what Congress meant by a "major life activity." Is dancing a major life activity? Reproducing? Singing? Reading? Graduating from college? Test taking? And how substantial is "substantial?" We would all agree that someone who could not walk is substantially limited in a major life activity. But what about someone who can walk but not run? Is that person substantially limited? Or how about someone who can read the newspaper but not a textbook? Or can see, but not well enough to meet FAA vision requirements for commercial pilots? Is Jonathan Love substantially impaired because he can take a test but not score high enough to gain easy admission to a top-tier law school?

Many other questions emerged as employers and others were faced with ADA compliance. Is someone disabled if he is severely near-sighted but has normal vision with glasses (considered under the ADA a "mitigating measure")? Is the employer entitled to request verification of the disability? Who pays for that evaluation? Is a doctor's diagnosis a sufficient basis for identifying someone as disabled? Does the employer have the right to reject a claim of disability? What form of grievance procedures is considered sufficient? What metric should be used to establish whether someone is substantially impaired? Can it be based on a person's educational level or socioeconomic status? This litany of questions represents only a small subset of those that have arisen over the years.

Defining the group of individuals covered under the ADA is far more challenging than it is for other civil rights legislation. The so-called "protected class" under the Civil Rights Act of 1964 is more easily identified given that the markers (race, color, religion, sex, and national origin) are generally straightforward. So, too, is the Age Discrimination in Employment Act, because it sets the age of forty as the cut-point for coverage under the law. What constitutes a disability is a thornier question than what characterizes a person as female, Native American, or Buddhist.

When Congress passes a law, a federal agency is assigned to generate and enforce regulations, practices, and policies. For the ADA, Congress assigned those tasks to an agency within the Department of Justice, the U.S. Equal Employment Opportunity Commission (EEOC). Beginning in July of 1991 the EEOC began to publish a series of guidelines and policies. The document relevant to the implementation of Title III alone runs some 230 pages and over 100,000 words as it specifies issues like what constitutes a shopping center, the height of sinks in restrooms, the minimum pulse time for a visual emergency alarm, and who pays for attorney fees if lawsuits are brought to court.

The keystone document, with the unassuming title of "Part 36—Nondiscrimination on the Basis of Disability by Public Accommodations and in Commercial Facilities," offers guidelines directly relevant to decisions surrounding test accommodations. Of particular importance is the clarification it offers regarding what constitutes a significant impairment in a major life activity. According to the policy, "The phrase major life activities means functions such as caring for one's self, performing manual tasks, walking, seeing, hearing, speaking, breathing, learning, and working." The EEOC's understanding of Congressional intent emphasizes that major life activities are fundamental capacities required for normal adaptation. Dancing is not a major life activity, nor likely is being able to draw. But is test taking?

The EEOC guidelines also present this amplification: "A person is considered an individual with a disability . . . when the individual's important life activities are restricted as to the conditions, manner, or duration under which they can be performed in comparison to most people. A person with a minor, trivial impairment, such as a simple infected finger, is not impaired in a major life activity. A person who can walk for ten miles continuously is not substantially limited in walking merely because, on the eleventh mile, he or she begins to experience pain, because most people would not be able to walk eleven miles without experiencing some discomfort." In this statement, the EEOC seems to have set the metric for how to judge disability. It stated that a person's level of functioning should be evaluated by comparing it to what was typical of "most people," what some of us have referred to as the "average person standard." Nothing in the wording suggests that the comparison group should be individuals of like intelligence, level of education, socioeconomic status, or profession. Simply put, the ADA was intended to protect people who, when compared to those in the general population, are unable to perform routine activities that are central to normal daily living.

Establishing the average person as the litmus test for gauging impairment has far-reaching implications that are not always easy to swallow, especially for those relatively well-functioning individuals who want the law to allow for special consideration. If a college or test organization chooses to hold the line, the law and attendant regulations would support a narrowing of the definition of disability to include only those who are truly abnormal relative to most people. As I alluded to earlier, however, the ADA does not force an institution to abide by the average person standard. It only sets the average person as the legal yardstick.

Another pillar of the ADA's conceptual foundation is its stated intent to ensure access, not success. Nowhere in this law or the ensuing policies will you find language that frames accommodations as a tool to maximize a person's outcome. The ADA is not about guaranteeing that an individual with a disability should, to paraphrase an Army slogan, "Be all that he can be." Nor is it intended purely to "level the playing field," despite the common association of that metaphor with the ADA. The law is more about giving somebody *access* to the playing field. It simply says that someone who is otherwise qualified to do a job should be able to work at that job even if he or she has a disability that, while substantial, does not hinder performing the job's essential functions. If I'm a perfectly capable therapist, I should be able to compete for an opening at a clinic even though that clinic might have to install a wheelchair ramp should they hire me. However, that clinic is not required to make sure that I am a successful therapist. My success or failure as an employee would be up to me.

The spirit of the ADA's stated intent also wafts through the EEOC policy on test accommodations. Section 36.309 "requires that a private entity offering an examination covered by the section must assure that the examination is selected and administered so as to best ensure that the examination accurately reflects an individual's aptitude or achievement level or other factor the examination purports to measure, rather than reflecting the individual's impaired sensory, manual, or speaking skills (except where those skills are the factors that the examination purports to measure)." If a person who was legally blind wanted to take the SAT, he should be provided with a Braille or auditory version of the test because it is not intended to measure how well someone can see; it is intended to measure verbal and math skills. Forcing someone with a visual handicap to take a standard paper and pencil version would be discriminatory because his score would reflect the impact of his disability, not the level of his skills.

By the same token, the person with a visual handicap would not be entitled to accommodations on a vision test administered to obtain a driver's license. Because the test is designed to measure visual acuity, any accommodations would fundamentally alter the test itself. For example, it would not make sense to allow a person with a severe visual handicap the accommodation of having a sighted person read the eye chart for him. The highways could be choked by accidents involving blind people with licenses to drive.

To bring the analogy somewhat closer to the realm of higher education: Let's say someone with a bona fide reading disability wanted accommodations to take a reading test. Because the test "purports" to measure reading, it would be hard to imagine that the EEOC would require the test administrator to provide the examinee a person to read for him. Again, the ADA is about giving you the opportunity to succeed, not the circumstances that will assure success at all costs.

The idea that the ADA is outcome-neutral is a hard one for many to understand and accept. Of the last twenty-five documentation packets I have read, seventeen contain a statement by the examinee and/or clinician akin to the following: "This student requires accommodations so that he can perform at his best on the exam." A report I just read had this sentence: "Joseph is entitled to extra time as a way to ensure that his test scores match his superior IQ." In a personal statement, Joseph wrote, "I would like my LSAT score to be an accurate reflection of all the motivation and talent I embody." Inherent in these statements is the idea that ADA is designed to secure maximal performance.

Joseph and his clinician are not alone in their misconstrual of the ADA. In 2002 my colleagues and I published a survey of clinicians about their understanding of the law. A third of a sample of 147 clinicians who had submitted documentation on behalf of students seeking legal accommodations agreed with the statement, "The ADA was intended by Congress to help individuals with disabilities improve their academic success and testing performance." Incidentally, over 40 percent said this statement was true: "Under the ADA, clinicians should determine impairment by comparing a patient's test scores with norms for students at similar educational levels."

Clinicians have a legitimate excuse for any misunderstandings they may harbor regarding ADA's intent. Most of us involved in the assessment of disabilities/disorders have as our reference point the special education laws that have evolved over the past thirty years. Their most recent incarnation, the Individuals with Disabilities Education Improvement Act of 2004 (IDEIA), represents an expansion and revision of the well-known Public Law 94-142 (the Education for All Handicapped Children Act) that legislated funding for special educational services in the "least restrictive environment." Both of these laws entitle handicapped children to a free and appropriate education *designed to optimize their achievement.* These statutes propel school districts across the country to provide (either within the district or at an independent facility) a range of special educational services, from resource rooms and inclusion classrooms, to self-contained programs and residential care. The laws entitle students with disabilities to support services that correct or circumvent deficiencies as well as remove barriers to learning. As stated in the 2006 Department of Education regulations implementing the latest revision of IDEIA, the purpose of the law is to "mobilize resources so that a child can learn as effectively as possible in his or her educational program." These laws therefore move beyond guaranteeing ADA-type civil rights protections; they require that schools identify individuals with disabilities and provide them with services that will maximize outcome.

The No Child Left Behind Act (NCLB) of 2001, signed by President George W. Bush, reinforces the commitment to assist students with disabilities by requiring accountability of performance. It assures that, where possible, students with disabilities should meet the basic academic benchmarks set for students in regular education. Consequently, all students, regardless of disability status, are compared on similar standardized measures. Test accommodations are provided to facilitate improvement in academic performance for low achievers who meet certain standards. Both IDEIA and NCLB seek to optimize academic outcomes for students, including those with disabilities. In this regard, these laws promote advocacy for those with special needs by mandating educational resources, such as test accommodations. And, as such, they represent a different kettle of fish when compared to the Americans with Disabilities Act.

Differences in intent between special education laws and the ADA serve to frustrate and confuse students, parents, and clinicians. It is hard for them to understand how students can be considered in need of special services through high school but lose that designation in college or when they apply for test accommodations on a post-graduate examination. However, that scenario is not only conceivable but entirely possible, especially given the wide range of criteria school districts might use for identifying a need for special education.

After regulatory agencies publish rules for the enactment of a law, the legal system takes over the effort to provide clarifications and consequences. That process is patchwork, unpredictable, oftentimes contradictory from jurisdiction to jurisdiction, case specific, and foggy even when the Supreme Court issues rulings intended to bring coherence to the disparate opinions issued by lower courts.

The body of law surrounding the ADA is especially riddled with sore spots and irritations. Reviewing these opinions now, even those limited to test accommodations, is more than a non-lawyer should have to endure, at least at this juncture in the account of Jonathan Love's time in court. Yet it is important to establish that, to date, courts have generally affirmed the bedrock principles of the law I have described. As for the definition of disability, they have consistently supported the view that one is covered under the law only if the degree of impairment is substantial. More importantly, they have made it clear that "substantial impairment" is determined by what is typical of most people, that is, the average person in the population.

The ADA has been in force for enough time that even the Supreme Court has weighed in on the definition of disability. Affirming rulings of multiple federal district judges and the EEOC guidelines, the Supreme court in 1999 declared in the case of *Sutton et al.* v. *United Air Lines, Inc.*: "The term 'substantially limits' means, among other things, '[u]nable to perform a major life activity that the average person in the general population can perform;' or '[s]ignificantly restricted as to the condition, manner or duration under which an individual can perform a particular major life activity as compared to the condition, manner, or duration under which the average person in the general population can perform that same major life activity." This ruling seems to undercut the contention that a graduate student, for example, could be considered disabled simply because he was unable to perform as well as other graduate students on a high-stakes examination. Most people in the general population are not even in contention for postgraduate education. In fact, roughly 75 percent of the population never completes a four-year college degree. Therefore, graduate students are not the average person.

As a consequence, the courts have confirmed that the ADA should be viewed as an antidiscrimination act, not as an entitlement for individuals whose problems are troublesome, but not overwhelming. It also means that a Jonathan Love's functioning should be judged against norms for the general population, not against what one might expect of individuals vying for places in prestigious law schools.

The Supreme Court not only validated the average person standard, but it also narrowed the definition of disability to include only those people who were currently and substantially impaired whether or not they were treated for the disability. In the case of *Sutton et al.* v. *United Air Lines, Inc.*, the Supreme Court wrote, "the language is properly read as requiring that a person be presently—not potentially or hypothetically—substantially limited in order to demonstrate a disability. A 'disability' exists only where an impairment 'substantially limits' a major life activity, not where it 'might,' 'could,' or 'would' be substantially limiting if corrective measures were not taken." With this language, the court rejected the argument that one could be disabled even if current treatment or self-accommodations allowed for normal adjustment. For example, a person could not say, "I'm disabled under the ADA because, without my glasses, I can't see." This ruling made it clear that determination of disability should be based on a person's current level of impairment, with relative disregard to the various treatments, compensations, or assistive devices (i.e., mitigating measures) that allowed for that level of functioning.

This case has other implications for those of us clinicians who are involved in disability determinations. First, it draws a clear distinction between having a clinical diagnosis and a legal disability. For instance, I carry a diagnosis of myopia because, without my contact lenses, I am legally blind (somewhere around 20/400). However, when I wear my contact lenses, I am corrected to 20/20. Under the law, I am not disabled because, with mitigating measures, I can see as well as most people. The same principle can apply in psychiatric conditions: A person who legitimately meets criteria for ADHD may not meet the legal standard if, with medication, he functions at least as well as most people.

The Court's ruling on mitigating measures has other direct consequences for individuals who seek test accommodations based on psychiatric or learning disorders. It significantly undermines the argument that someone can be considered disabled if he has to work harder or compensate more than others in an educational program. The ADA, as interpreted by the courts, makes it clear that the basis for judging disability is the level of current impairment in handling routine circumstances when compared to the average person.

The Supreme Court also clarified the scope of a "significant impairment in a major life activity" under the ADA. In the case of *Toyota Motor Manufacturing, Kentucky, Inc. v. Williams*, an employee with carpal tunnel syndrome filed a claim of discrimination against the car manufacturer; she contended that they had not sufficiently accommodated her disability. While a lower court sided with Toyota's claim that she was not disabled under the ADA definition, a court of appeals found that she had satisfied criteria for disability because her injuries prevented her from doing manual tasks associated with certain types of assembly line jobs.

In a unanimous opinion delivered by Justice Sandra Day O'Connor, the Supreme Court reversed and dismissed the case, holding that it is not sufficient under the ADA for an employee to simply offer evidence of a medical diagnosis of impairment. Instead, evidence must be offered that the limitations caused by the employee's medical condition are of "central importance to the daily lives of most people." The Supreme Court found that the kinds of tasks this employee could not manage (those that involved repetitive work requiring the hands and arms to extend above shoulder level for prolonged periods of time) did not constitute an important part of most people's daily lives. The high court noted that she could still perform certain household chores despite her impairments, including tending to her personal hygiene and carrying out other basic domestic duties. The justices wrote: "Household chores, bathing, and brushing one's teeth, in contrast, are among the types of manual tasks of central importance to people's daily lives." The high court set a high standard for what could be considered impairment sufficient to warrant protection under the ADA.

When I first read the newspaper account of that 2002 opinion, I phoned one of my fellow consultants to notify him that our stint as documentation reviewers for test accommodations requests would soon be up. If the benchmark for determining a physical disability was brushing one's teeth and bathing, surely the analog for a learning/psychiatric disability would be similarly elemental. We gathered that the major life activity of learning entailed the capacity to acquire skills fundamental to daily life, such as figuring out a bus schedule or reading cooking directions. To be considered as disabled by symptoms associated with ADHD, we assumed that someone would have to prove that he was unable to organize himself to get laundry done, groceries purchased, bills paid, children to school, and simple work tasks completed. Surely, any judge would recognize that being able to take the LSAT or the Step examinations for medical licensing involved abilities worlds removed from the learning equivalent of bathing and brushing one's teeth. Who would pursue test accommodations and legal recourse after the Supreme Court so bluntly narrowed the definition of disability? Wrong again.

In a way, the Supreme Court was delimiting legal disability in a manner similar to how Dr. Jerome Wakefield, a professor of social work at New York University, has been advocating over many years for mental disorders. According to Wakefield, a disorder represents a "harmful dysfunction" in a set of mental mechanisms required for successful adaptation. Wakefield's definition requires the problem to be serious enough that it can lead to death, illness, and/or impairments in major life activities. By major life activities, he means human functions that, through the course of evolution, have proven necessary for survival. These might include being able to interact productively with others in a social group and organize oneself sufficiently to allow for task completion. Like the Supreme Court, Wakefield wants clinicians to focus on the extent to which someone is impaired in the ability to manage fundamental demands of daily life.

The impact of the Supreme Court's ventures into disability law has had an impact on other decisions. In one case especially relevant to *Love* v. *LSAC*, a medical student by the name of Michael Gonzales sued the National Board of Medical Examiners because they denied him the accommodations on the first "step" of the licensing examination. A district court had ruled that the documentation did not support the student's claim he had a reading disability because the "Plaintiff's performance in both reading and writing tests fell within the average to superior range when compared to most people." A federal appeals court, citing the Supreme Court's trio of decisions, upheld the lower court's ruling. The justices wrote: "Average, or even slightly below average, is not disabled for purposes of the ADA." Once again, the definition of disability has been narrowed considerably, thereby widening the gap between legal and clinical definitions of a disorder.

For years I held to the accepted notion that the standards a clinician uses to judge impairment should be held distinct from those that apply to the ADA. In my mind, these were two different worlds with two different sets of goals, methods, and benchmarks. We clinicians were about helping people who had, or thought they had, problems in some aspect of their lives. Our job was to work with clients to identify those problems and fix them without worrying too much about the extent to which they impaired functioning. If a person felt he had a problem, he likely had a problem of one sort or another. Was it not problematic that someone with a superior IQ was only able to earn average grades in his high school English classes? Should we not help the spacey little girl who, while generally competent, never got herself ready in time for school or completed chores without ample parental prodding? From my pre-ADA perspective, a patient's presenting complaints need not be monumental to warrant formal psychological identification and treatment.

Besides, if you limited the assignment of diagnoses just to those who were abnormal in substantial ways, what would happen to business for all of us mental health providers? Judging from our research, we would be reducing our customer base by two-thirds, at least. That is all we need the already recalcitrant insurance companies to hear: "You don't really need to be paying for relatively well-functioning people to get psychiatric services. From now on we're going to assign formal diagnoses only to those with problems that, when compared to most people, are substantial. Happy? Look at all the money you're saving!"

I kept the clinical and legal worlds in separate orbits until I became more involved in ADA-oriented documentation reviews. Gradually I began to wonder whether the law might not have gotten it right. For sure, it was much cleaner to define abnormality relative to the average person than to a range of standards based upon IQ status, educational levels, and estimates of potential. To my concrete mind, it became hard to justify diagnostic standards that fluctuated depending on how talented you were, the educational programs you pursued, or the expectations people had for you based on their sense of your prospects. I knew that physicians did not follow that scheme in their evaluations of medical disorders. A torn ligament is a torn ligament, regardless of how good an athlete the patient was prior to tearing his ligament. A concussion is a concussion, no matter how good the victim's memory was prior to the blow. Doctors would lose their licenses if they diagnosed healthy people as having medical problems based not on abnormal functioning relative to most people but, instead, on how much better the patient could function if he had medical assistance.

It also dawned on me that identifying high-functioning individuals as disabled had a range of unintended consequences, many of which I never considered in my role as a clinician. But those downsides became conspicuous once I thought about what happens when you open the gates of abnormality to the pathologically average. Certainly it has the effect of limiting access to scarce resources for the functionally impaired. In the zero sum game of disability services, every special educator assigned to a college-bound student with relatively weak but still average reading abilities is one less teacher for the student with dim prospects for graduating high school because he cannot read. If clinics limited services for ongoing treatment to those clients who were significantly maladjusted, waiting lists for mental health services would shrink overnight. In the context of a severe nationwide shortage of mental health services for all age groups and disorders, should we not allocate resources to those who are most impaired? And how fair is it that the rest of us should have to fund services (through taxes, tuition costs, and insurance premiums) to maximize the success of relatively normal people? The inequality is especially frustrating in that, according to a November 8, 2003, *New York Times* article, affluent districts have a far higher rate of accommodations (in this case, on the SAT) than large urban districts.

I had other reasons for my incremental change of heart. I thought more about the other students in the examination room who had to compete with individuals who were granted extra time based on questionable determinations. How fair was it to those other examinees, many of whom might not even be as intelligent or talented as the accommodated student? Was it right that some students were able to seek accommodations mainly because they had the financial means for an evaluation (rather than because they were more impaired than others)? This fairness issue became all the more personal to me as my own children began to take entrance examinations like the SAT and LSAT.

It is also not hard to spin a societal cost for feeding the notion that a bright person is disabled if he has trouble accomplishing lofty goals easily. Is it good for a society to consider every variation in human abilities as a basis for disability-based entitlements? What does it say for us as a nation when parents cannot accept that, contrary to the Lake Wobegon Effect, not all of our children are above average? Might we be headed toward the cliff's edge when we become comfortable with medicating children not because they have a disorder, but because we want to maximize their performance?

In my clinical work, I also began to see what happens when normal children are pathologized for perceived underperformance. How good is it for a child to walk around thinking he has a learning disability or a psychiatric problem when, in reality, he is not doing all that poorly (albeit theoretically less well than he might)? The case we had just yesterday in our ADHD clinic is all too typical: A thoroughly charming and talented eighth grader I will call Abby found herself in a psychiatry clinic because her parents were convinced she had ADHD. While Abby may not be the most organized, attentive, and academically-oriented child on Earth, she was no slouch academically in that she managed average grades in a rigorous private school. Her average intellectual abilities in concert with a preference for singing and dancing over algebra and Earth science drained her reservoir of attention quickly. But she did fine for herself in every way, notwithstanding her parents' contention that her grades would improve if she only paid better attention.

Their pursuit of a psychiatric evaluation, however, was not without its consequences. While well-intentioned, they conveyed to their daughter a message she had already internalized deeply: she was a disappointment. It did not help that her older sister was an academic superstar in the same school. During the interview Abby talked about how anxious she felt around her school-work, how intensely frustrated her mother became with her, and how she hoped she really did not have ADHD because that could make matters even worse. As she put it to the interviewer, "That's all I need is for my parents to think I'm even more of a loser than they already think I am." It was hard for us to hear that a visit to our clinic represented to this delightful young girl further evidence that she was lacking.

Some parents use psychiatric diagnosis far more destructively. To avoid facing up to their own problems or misdeeds, they campaign to establish their child's purported psychiatric disorder as the single explanation for all that is bad in their world. No matter how obvious it is that the family is a cauldron of chaos because of severe marital problems, parental mental illness, or perhaps domestic violence, they struggle to keep the focus on their child's supposed bipolar disorder or ADHD. They are broadcasting to all who will listen: "What do you expect from me? This child is so out of control that there's no way I can make things better. In fact, you should pity me for being saddled with such a mentally ill child." The idea that the child's behavior might be an expectable reaction to a horrendous environment rather than the consequences of a psychiatric disorder is verboten. The moment a therapist might try to focus on those non-child issues, the parent will become hostile, might well miss the next session, or bolt altogether in search of a more "understanding" clinician. Unfortunately, all too many therapists are quick to comply with this sort of psychiatric Munchausen by proxy. It certainly is easier to treat a child's faux-bipolar disorder with medication than it is to confront reactive parents with a more accurate formulation.

Two personal experiences pushed me especially hard toward the legal metric for determining what constitutes a clinical disorder. The first was a case I reviewed for the National Board of Medical Examiners (NBME) involving a medical student I will call Katy. She sought extra time on the board exams because she had failed past administrations. With the support of several prominent clinicians and a team of lawyers, she claimed that her inability to pass the test was tied to her ADHD and learning disabilities. A hearing was held in federal court because, based on the ADA, she was seeking a temporary restraining order against the NBME that would force it to grant accommodations.

As for some details of the case: Katy was admitted to a fully-accredited, US-based medical school located in a major city. How she gained admission to medical school is puzzling because she had never been a good student. According to the record, she required extensive tutoring in order to earn Bs and Cs in elementary school. Her SAT scores all fell below the 10th percentile according to national norms. Her scores on the Medical School Admission Test (MCAT) were also extremely low. Yet she somehow was accepted into medical school under a program that allowed her extra time to complete the basic courses. Unfortunately, Katy could not pass her exams despite intensive effort and assistance. She and the clinicians she consulted concluded that her academic problems were associated with a reading disability and ADHD.

The psychological testing completed by her psychologists painted a sadly different picture. The profiles depicted a person with limited intellectual abilities who must have studied ferociously to make it through high school and college. Her full scale IQ was 80, a score that falls at the 9th percentile for the general population (an IQ score of 100 is average). While her verbal IQ of 91 was in the low end of the average range, her performance IQ of 72 represents a borderline retarded score. Given that most medical students have measured full scale IQs around 125, Kathy was at a monumental disadvantage. It is no wonder that she found it hard to complete work as quickly and accurately as her classmates. Also predictable were her reports of being frustrated, distressed, anxious, and depressed. Imagine trying to be successful and at ease when all your time is devoted to mastering material far beyond your abilities.

Almost ten years later, I still remember how uncomfortable it was to testify in front of this student and her family. I had to explain to the judge in open court that Katy's problems in medical school were a predictable consequence of her cognitive limitations. If anything, her academic progress was a testament to qualities inconsistent with ADHD: persistence, attention, and an unusual capacity for hard work. I explained that the diagnosis of ADHD was never intended to cover scenarios whereby an individual's talents were outstripped by aspirations. I also told the judge that, as far as I knew, the ADA did not guarantee a medical license for absolutely anyone who wanted to be a physician, even if that person had significant intellectual limitations. The judge ultimately agreed with that position.

The hearing produced testimony that I found even more thought provoking than the diagnostic or legal issues at play. I learned that Katy had spent over four years of her life and untold amounts of money on tuitions, tutors, and lawyers in her quest to pursue a dream she had absolutely no chance of realizing. Witnesses and affidavits spoke admiringly of the lengths to which she went to handle the curriculum, for example, locking herself in a room for days at a time trying to understand biochemistry or anatomy. She claimed to have eschewed all socializing for years so as not to distract from her studies. By all accounts, her determination was legion.

How sad for Katy that none of the many clinicians and specialists she consulted leveled with her. Instead, they told her what she wanted to hear even though her intellectual weaknesses had been well documented. Psychiatric diagnosis and disability law served to derail her from finding a job more suited to her talents. All those years of tireless effort went for nothing other than a mountain of aggravation and disappointment. It struck me at that time how much better it would have been for Katy had clinicians not set her up to fail by repackaging her marginal academic skills as a reflection of disability. Her deans and professors would have also served her better had they not played to her fantasy of becoming a physician.

The second experience that changed my thinking about clinical versus legal definitions of disability arose from a workshop I presented at a national meeting for a support group devoted to ADHD in adults. During one of the breaks, I walked around the exhibit hall that had been set up in the hotel ballroom. Among the familiar booths hosted by publishing and pharmaceutical companies was a collection of exhibits selling products essentially bestowing the virtues of having ADHD. One gentleman with guitar in hand hawked a CD of songs he had written to let the world know that ADHD was a gift, not a curse. Another offered a book that explained how ADHD allowed for effective multitasking, creative problem solving, and powerful intuitions. Still others presented materials that characterized ADHD as a disorder that benefited the busy executive.

When I took a closer look at the conference program, I saw that my workshop promoting the benefits of diagnostic rigor was anomalous. This meeting was not about the diagnosis and treatment of a psychiatric disorder. It was more a celebration of ADHD. The conference room right next to mine featured a workshop with a title something akin to, "ADHD: The Hidden Gift." I later learned that the presenter offered strategies for helping spouses and bosses appreciate the unique talents associated with having this disorder. Many other seminars also fêted symptoms as joys.

In the vernacular of my youth, this atmosphere was mind-blowing and not a little disturbing. I knew from years of experience seeing patients and reading the research literature that having ADHD was a burden, not an advantage, particularly when it came to managing educational opportunities and jobs. What patients experienced as a consequence of having ADHD never fell in the realm of a hidden gift or capacity for multitasking. They dealt with daily reminders that others considered them to be screw-ups and losers. As a group, they were more prone to be fired for poor job performance and misconduct, more likely to become involved in serious accidents, and experience a range of other psychiatric problems. None of the patients I treated would concur with the romanticized view of ADHD as a blessing.

Whenever I have encountered efforts to glorify psychiatric symptoms, I am always of mixed mind. I would imagine that some with a disorder are heartened when others tout the fruits that abnormality can bear. Extreme short stature can be an advantage for jockeys, a talent for hallucinating a prerequisite for shamans, and extreme obsessiveness can have value for an auditor. Turning weaknesses to strengths is a fundamental element of effective problem solving.

Alas, every upside is paired with a doppelganger headed in the opposite direction. Cheerleading for the joys of having a psychiatric disorder is no exception. If a disorder bestows substantial benefits, is it really a disorder? Can you imagine people with other disorders, psychiatric or physical, singing songs about the thrill of being depressed or having lung cancer? How are we supposed to encourage skeptical educators, managed care administrators, parents, politicians, judges, and physicians to take the disorder seriously if they all hear that ADHD is an enabling disability? If we water down the concept of a disorder to the point that symptoms represent an advantage, why should insurance companies pay for care or school principals support special educational services? How am I supposed to get services for my truly impaired adult patient with ADHD if everyone considers it a cheap excuse for securing an advantage? I thought then, as I do now, that those who portray ADHD as a plus might not be considering some of the lurking minuses on the horizon.

In case you suspect that I am erecting straw men, surf to www.addexecutive. com. This Web site, devoted to executives with Attention Deficit Disorder (ADD), describes its mission as follows: "For better and worse, we've got the magic ADD. One moment we're right here, and the next we're hey, check out this new online tool for Jim, would you double check the figures on the KRX proposal? The ADD executive is here to serve us (and our colleagues) who believe that ADD is something to be taken advantage of where it's an asset, and managed where it isn't." The site features a host of articles about ADD treatments and management strategies.

Or head over to http://www.additudemag.com/adhd/article/754.html where you will find the article, "Adult ADHD in the corner office: How 5 top executives transformed their attention deficit disorder into an asset in the workplace." You will learn how Paul Orfalea, founder of the copying empire, Kinko's, and David Neeleman, founder and CEO of JetBlue Airways, used their ADHD as "assets on their respective career paths."

Now imagine you are an employer or insurance company executive and you read about these highly successful executives who claim to have ADHD. What would your reaction be? Would you say, "Jeez, this is a pretty serious disorder that research has demonstrated to cause serious impairment in an individual's capacity to adjust," or would you think otherwise? Might you not say, "What kind of silliness is that? If the owner of a major airline claims to have ADHD, how could he be that successful? Isn't this whole ADHD deal a little bogus? Why is being a little disorganized or inattentive suddenly a psychiatric disorder that can warrant federal entitlements?" By confusing personality style with mental illness, these articles skew public perceptions in ways that, in my opinion, are counterproductive. To quote one of my patients when I told him about the conference program, "Anyone who's walking around saying how good it is to have ADHD definitely doesn't have ADHD. It sucks."

I had one other concern as I strolled through ADHD in Wonderland and talked to the attendees. It was clear to me that many of them defined themselves by their disorder. They were their ADHD. How did they come to be a real estate agent? Because of ADHD. Why did their husband want a divorce?

Because of ADHD. How is it they are interested in music and art? Because of ADHD. Why don't they like to cook? Because of ADHD. The unifying principle for understanding their lives was derived from the pages of the DSM.

Even if some of these people met criteria for the disorder, I am not sure you would want to encourage an ADHD-centric self view. Most people resist being defined by their illnesses, and for good reason. They prefer not to see themselves as "John the Cancer Patient" but as "John, the Father of Three, Who is an Excellent Accountant and Lifelong Dead Head Who also has Cancer." The politically correct form for writing about disorders reflects this sentiment. Journal editors will swap the words "ADHD Children" for "Children with ADHD" in every instance. While it can make for some awkward sentence construction, it does drive the point home.

The impact of fostering "identity by disorder" is most palpable in children. I wince when I hear parents refer to their "ADHD child" or, even more so, when a youngster says, "I'm ADHD." About the last thing parents should want for their child is for him or her to have a disorder-based identity. Even for children who really are impaired, what better way to foster a sense of dependence and diminished responsibility than to inculcate an identity based on his disability? And in the case of a capable youngster who has been labeled as having ADHD based on dubious criteria, what must that be like for him? Do you want to communicate to a high-functioning child that he has a mental illness not because he is doing so poorly but because he could be doing even better? Or if he knows full well that his brain is just fine except that he has to deal with an intensively reactive mother or parents who fight or a father who becomes increasingly aggressive with each beer? While diagnoses can pave the way for necessary services, they also can cause harm when they are justified poorly or reified unfairly.

As the downsides of overly-enthusiastic diagnosis became clearer to me, I found myself increasingly enamored with the idea of applying the legal definition of disability to clinical circumstances. I became more aware that the therapist's impulse toward patient advocacy has unintended consequences many of us ignore. And I felt all the more comfortable testifying in trials like Love v. LSAC. While I could not understand why Judge Surrick chose not to throw the case out the moment he heard Jonathan Love earned an average score on the LSAT under standard testing conditions and possessed four letters of admission to law school, I was not entirely unhappy with his decision. At least the "Not Every Diagnosis is a Disability" view might have its day in court.

CHAPTER 4

Depositions

My first stint as an expert witness charted the course for all depositions, hearings, and trials to follow. In the mid-1990s a university's attorney asked me to provide testimony regarding the proper assessment of ADHD. The lawyer summoned me to Boston the night before to prepare me for the next day's legal wranglings. I needed that instruction in the worst way. Graduate programs teach aspiring clinical psychologists all manner of knowledge and skills. We learn about neurophysiology, abnormal psychology, child development, statistics, methodology, experimental design, diagnostic assessment, systems of psychotherapy, outcomes research, and program evaluation. In our clinical practica we learn how to administer/interpret psychological testing, manage the full range of psychiatric disorders, and maximize therapeutic benefit via evidence based practice. We take classes, participate in seminars, and travel for placements and internships. We spend endless hours kowtowing to professors, site supervisors, and departmental secretaries. But nowhere along the way does anyone explain how to survive hours-long sparring sessions with lawyers bent on establishing, for the record, that you are an idiot, and an untrustworthy one at that.

My ignorance as an expert witness extended beyond the technicalities of a deposition. Not long after I agreed to participate, I read Jonathan Harr's gripping bestseller, *A Civil Action*, which documents a 1979 trial involving the town of Woburn, Massachusetts. A group of families convince an otherwise cynical personal injury lawyer (played by John Travolta in the movie) to take on several conglomerates they contended were responsible for contaminating the drinking water and causing unusually high rates of childhood leukemia. Expert witnesses were aplenty, some sinister, others decent, but all subject to withering cross-examinations from opposing counsel. It did not take much imagination to put myself in their shoes, experience a rush of apprehension, and wonder exactly what it was that I was thinking when I agreed to participate. It did not help at all that the trial involving the university would take place in the exact same federal courthouse as the one Harr portrayed in his book. I arrived in Boston uninformed and anxious.

The advice the university's attorney gave me via lecture and videotape made exquisite sense not just for depositions but for conversations in general. Most elements of the instructions were anchored in common sense: I was to discipline myself to listen carefully to the entire question before responding. Under no circumstances should I utter a word in reply unless I was absolutely certain I understood the question. If I did not understand the question (or thought it was stated in such a way as to make impossible an unambiguous answer), I was to ask the lawyer to restate it. My responses should be simple, direct, and truthful. I was to avoid losing my temper, volunteering information that fell outside the line of inquiry, and expressing opinions without being supremely confident I could defend them during trial. As best I could tell, I was to adopt a stance similar to one they recommend to prisoners of war subject to brutal interrogation.

Other aspects of the deposition training session were more unique to this legal process. I was to understand that a deposition was part of the "discovery" phase of a trial when each side has the opportunity to see all the evidence that will come before the judge. Unlike TV versions of trials, those in real life (and especially at a federal level) have no surprise witnesses or dramatic last-second introductions of smoking guns. Evidence is pursued and disclosed for all to see, question, and interpret.

To prepare their case, each side can query opposing witnesses for what they might testify at trial. They can use the deposition transcript to build their arguments against your position, formulate a cross examination that impeaches the accuracy of your statements, and trip you up if, at trial, you say anything the least inconsistent with what you indicated in the deposition. For example, if in the deposition you indicate that the prevalence of ADHD is 3-5 percent but at trial you say 3–7 percent (perhaps because, in the intervening months new data were published), a sharp attorney will highlight the discrepancy as a way of raising questions about your expertise. If you cite an article as supporting your position that is actually of dubious relevance, you will hear about it at trial. Depositions are lousy places to overstate research findings as a way of making points.

Familiar with nervous witnesses, the attorney assured me that most of his fellow lawyers find it worthwhile to be gentle and conversational during depositions. Most are wary of asking questions that might tip the hand they might play at trial by way of strategy and counterargument. They probably also want to save the rhetorical fireworks for the judge, preferring to use the deposition to probe your position for future attack.

Now fully prepared and after a restless evening, I made my way to the office of the attorney who was hosting the deposition. My mentor lawyer was in attendance alongside a court reporter and the opposing counsel. The latter was a middle-aged fellow with a ring of coppery gray hair, wire-rimmed glasses, and a friendly face. After a few minutes of chitchat, I was sworn in (another reason to tell the truth, the whole truth, and nothing but the truth), answered a few questions about my place of residence, and settled in for the deposition to begin in earnest.

The first series of questions from the plaintiff's attorney were innocent enough. He asked where I worked, the overall nature of my research, and how I was contacted by the defense team. No problems so far. But once he approached the heart of the subject I was to testify about, he became anything but the conversational, gentle questioner my instructor had promised. He asked long and winding questions designed to lure me into responses that were easy to misconstrue. Remembering the advice from the prior evening, I asked him to repeat the question so I could answer straightforwardly. Although palpably exasperated that he had to start over again, he complied nonetheless.

After a few iterations of me asking for him to repeat questions, he became overtly frustrated with me. His face turned red, his shoulders hunched, and he leaned forward in his seat so that his face was close to mine. Most unnerving, however, was that The Vein of Death appeared on his forehead. It rose steadily above the surface of his skin, turned a deep purple hue, and pulsated as if it had taken on a life of its own. The more I refused to answer impenetrable questions, the harder The Vein did beat, to such a degree that I began to wonder about deposition protocol should the attorney suffer a sudden stroke. It did not help that he began to sweat profusely, spit his words toward me, and look as if he were ready to propel himself across the table.

At first I was taken aback that he should become so aggressive. Outside of marital circumstances, I was not used to this level of intense grilling. But it dawned on me that I knew exactly how to deal with someone acting like this lawyer. If my career prepared me for anything well, it was managing disruptive, antisocial youth who disregarded the normal rules of civility. And so I interacted with this lawyer as I would a conduct-disordered eighteen-year old or, better still, an eight-year-old in mid-tantrum. No matter how he sputtered and attacked, I looked him straight in the eye, kept my tone even, and acted as unflappably as one could in the presence of The Vein. Although I tried not to provoke him, I did not let him badger me either. He just needed to deal with the fact that I had no intention of letting him lead me down a road I chose not to travel.

After an hour of so of contentiousness, someone suggested that we take a break. That is when the most remarkable transformation occurred. We had not walked more than ten feet outside the conference room when smiles broke out all around, the conversation turned to the baseball standings, and The Vein receded to its lair. The attorney, who only minutes before had berated me with questions, now asked pleasantly about my trip to Boston, shared a personal anecdote about a visit to Syracuse, and spoke amiably with the opposing lawyer as if they were old friends (and, for all I know, they *were* old friends). No objections were raised, no biting sarcasm voiced. We were just working people on break.

As you might have expected, the camaraderie lasted precisely until the deposition hearing was reconvened, at which point The Vein returned to life. And that is when I came to appreciate that these interactions were not personal. It was business or, perhaps more accurately, sport to the attorneys. I am sure the opposing attorney could have cared less that I held opinions that were inconsistent with his theory of the case. He might even have agreed with me were he not hired to advocate for the other side. He did not know me well enough to judge whether I truly deserved his contempt. He was doing his job, I was doing mine, and it really did not matter to him who was right or wrong. It was about gathering ammunition for future combat.

With that experience as a backdrop, I have grown more comfortable about my intermittent forays into legal proceedings. It happens that attorneys I have encountered since the one who harbored The Vein have been far less belligerent with me. I have also come to realize that I hold certain advantages over the attorneys. While they know much more than I about the legalities of a hearing, I know far more about child psychiatric research and the accepted tenets of clinical practice. As long as I stick close to what I know to be accurate and supportable, I am going to be okay. You only get into trouble as an expert witness if you start offering opinions that are easily assailable. Credibility is the best defense against a successful legal attack.

I also have the advantage of feeling absolutely comfortable with the method I employ to judge documentation that examinees submit for accommodations. The criteria I use are based on consensus professional guidelines, the rationale for my recommendations are stated explicitly in the reports, and I would never suggest denial of accommodations unless I was absolutely convinced I was being fair. I definitely would never become involved in a legal proceeding unless I were 100 percent sure I was on the "right" side of the case. From my perspective, a courtroom is no place for an expert witness who is unable to be transparent and convincing in defending the logic of his position.

The cases that head toward court never fall into a gray zone. Those more debatable claims drop out of view well before they reach a judge's consideration. In fact, if the documentation is anywhere close to supporting accommodations, most of us consultants will recommend they be granted. No consultant would want to deny accommodations because of an impulse to nitpick on the number of symptoms required for a diagnosis or the validity of certain clinical judgments. If in doubt, we check the "Recommend Accommodations" box on the feedback form.

Because litigation is extraordinarily expensive, time consuming, and distracting, I believe that test organizations and academic institutions will only pursue the good and winnable fight. They would far prefer to settle those more subtle cases than risk money and prestige. Therefore, if someone like me is involved in litigation, chances are high that it falls in the "no-brainer" bin. It is the high school valedictorian with a stellar academic record who suddenly develops ADHD when his MCAT score is low or he opens the envelope notifying him that he failed the bar examination. Or the case might involve a medical student who is worried he might fail a medical board exam even though he has never failed a test in his life. When the dispute involves this type of scenario (as it usually does), confidence about testifying for the testing organization flows easily.

A final source of comfort derives from my personal work history. Because I am a clinician, researcher, and patient advocate, it is hard for an opposing attorney to peg me as a hostile ideologue bent on undermining the plight of the disabled. While I may believe in the benefits of some diagnostic rigor, I am not an anti-ADHD extremist who can be easily dismissed. Indeed, all the consultants I know have impeccable credentials. We spend far more time serving people with disabilities than reviewing ADA documentation. As I mentioned earlier, we all see ourselves as working to protect the rights of the truly disabled, not to violate them.

In the matter of *Jonathan Love* v. *LSAC*, my notice to prepare for deposition arrived in an e-mail from Jane Leopold-Leventhal, Esq., a partner in the law firm of Eastburn & Gray of Doylestown, Pennsylvania. Ms. Leopold-Leventhal had been hired to defend the LSAC by their corporate counsel, Joan VanTol, Esq. I learned later that these two attorneys had worked together on various matters over the course of ten years. Therefore, when

Mr. Weiner's Notice of Complaint arrived on Ms. VanTol's desk, she immediately called Eastburn & Gray for assistance.

On August 10, Ms. Leopold-Leventhal requested by e-mail my curriculum vita and a time we might talk. Later that day was the telephone conference with the judge when he set that extraordinarily short period for the "discovery" phase of the trial. His order set off a frenzy of activity for both sides. Subpoenas had to be issued, depositions set, documents gathered, and questions prepared. My deposition was only one of eleven conducted, most between September 1, and November 17 (the judge ultimately extended the window for discovery to allow for more than the initial thirty-day interval). Lawyers found themselves in the following destinations: Waco, Texas; Reno, Nevada; South Bend, Indiana; Shreveport, Louisiana; Berkeley, California; Syracuse, New York; and Newtown, Pennsylvania (home turf for the defendants).

My first conversation with the LSAC lawyers was relatively brief, focusing on possible dates for my deposition, the statement I had to prepare to submit prior to that event, and the general outline of the case. I let both of them know that, if they were interested, I could send materials about the diagnosis of ADHD and issues involved in determining impairment in students applying for accommodations. Given my prior forensic involvements, I had a packet at the ready with copies of book chapters, articles, and handouts designed to bring lawyers up to speed about issues they would likely know little about. I had found that it saved me hours on the phone if I had such a primer prepared for inquiring attorneys.

It took a court case or two for me to realize that the contribution of someone like me to the conduct of a legal proceeding could extend beyond simply stating facts or offering opinions. Most lawyers who become involved in cases like these are not experts in psychiatric diagnosis or clinical methods. The sum total of an attorney's knowledge about psychiatry might derive from an introductory psychology course in college or from reading magazine articles. They have no way of judging whether the plaintiff's clinicians followed professional guidelines, interpreted test scores appropriately, or arrived at sound conclusions. While they are able to formulate strategies based on legal arguments, they are often ill-prepared to devise coherent and informed questions to witnesses, their own or those on the opposing side.

Most attorneys will jump at the opportunity to learn from an expert who can educate them about clinical matters. To a person, those I have worked with are quick, eager, and motivated learners. They ask good questions, soak up every last detail, and quickly grasp the fundamental concepts involved. The time they have to become experts themselves is often measured in days rather than weeks, given that many of the proceedings are hastily called hearings.

The role of educator is, of course, a comfortable one for most of us who participate in these kinds of legal activities. All the consultants I work with are on the faculty of a medical school, college, university, or professional school. We know our subject matter and how to teach others who are new to the field. That is just what we do day in and day out through the years.

Whether in meetings behind the scenes or with lawyers before a judge, I learned that I was most helpful and at ease when I held to that role of educator. My function was not to argue a legal point, advocate for a client, or present myself as the Consummate Expert. I was involved to teach whoever wanted to learn about those areas in which I had expertise. In the trial of *Love* v. *LSAC*, I actually came to construe the entire process as an educational enterprise: We needed to teach the judge about ADHD and the life of Jonathan Love so that he might arrive at a reasonable conclusion as to whether the young man was disabled. I had to imagine that, if the judge understood the criteria for the diagnosis and used them to evaluate Mr. Love's personal history, he could only find in favor of the defense.

Within a few days of phone and e-mail interchanges, the LSAC lawyers indicated to me that they were eager to have me brief them on the scientific and clinical underpinnings of my opinion that Mr. Love was not psychiatrically impaired. While they had the intuition that his claim of disability had little merit, they were unclear how to undermine his case. In e-mails and phone conversations they wanted to know how professionals make the diagnosis, whether psychological testing was central to the determination, how clinicians assess the extent of impairment, whether the clinicians Mr. Love consulted were qualified and followed accepted practices, how someone with bona fide ADHD typically functioned in school or in social circumstances, and the probability that someone with ADHD could manage an MBA program at Notre Dame. I then started receiving the materials the lawyers began collecting from the opposing side: the reports Mr. Love's clinicians had prepared, the curriculum vitae of those clinicians, psychological test protocols, affidavits from interested parties, past report cards, and the like. The questions came at an increasingly rapid pace: Was this clinician right when she said you could have ADHD but still get mostly As in elementary school? What's a Processing Speed Disorder? Can someone fake a bad performance on the Nelson-Denny Reading Test? Is it more likely Jonathan has ADHD if his uncle was supposedly diagnosed with the disorder? Is it normal and accepted practice for a clinician to assign a diagnosis before she even gets records from the parents or school? And on and on. Within a short time, my role extended beyond potential witness to the defense team's resident ADHD consultant.

My first responsibility as a prospective witness was to prepare a statement for the court that presented my credentials, prior forensic experience, and rationale for recommending to LSAC that they deny Mr. Love's request for accommodations. These brief legal "declarations" by expert witnesses are intended to establish the credentials of the witness and lay out the general substance of the expected testimony. It also reports the expert's hourly and daily fee for testifying and consulting with the attorneys. The intent of this document is to give the opposing counsel an opportunity to find out who will be testifying and generally what they will be covering in that testimony.

My declaration, submitted on August 21, ran nine double-spaced pages of text plus an "exhibit" consisting of my curriculum vitae. The first two pages established my bona fides while the third described the process by which I came to review Love's documentation for the Law School Admission Council. The remainder of my declaration mostly restated the elements of the review I had submitted to the LSAC on August 1. I outlined the fundamental criteria for a DSM-IV diagnosis of ADHD. I also explained why the information submitted by Mr. Love in his application to the LSAC failed to support the contention that he met those criteria, given his life-long history of normal adjustment.

My declaration, while largely a redux of the initial documentation review, considered some new information the LSAC lawyers had received, including a "supplemental report" from Dr. Van Auken, the clinician who evaluated Jonathan Love in South Bend, Indiana. I also had a chance to read the declaration dated July 19, by the plaintiff's mother, Margaret Love. Her account led me to add the following:

> After my initial review, I had the opportunity to read the Declarations of Dr. Van Auken, as well as Margaret Love ("Mrs. Love") and Plaintiff, Jonathan Love, submitted in support of Plaintiff's Motion for Preliminary Injunction. The information contained in those declarations does not alter my original opinion. To the contrary, it provides further evidence of a normal childhood, benign educational history, and typical life adjustment. For example, his mother's decision to put him in kindergarten at age four belies the claim that he was severely hyperactive and distractible. It is highly unlikely that a parent would enroll a child early in kindergarten (or that a school would accept a child early) if he were unusually immature and dysregulated. Most schools ensure some degree of readiness prior to enrolling a four-year-old.
>
> It also is significant that, despite Margaret Love's obvious involvement and dedication to her son's progress, she never felt the need to consult her

pediatrician or a mental health/educational professional in an effort to manage his reported impairment. It seems likely that a referral was unnecessary because she and the teachers were able to manage him by using common classroom management and study techniques of the sort that many children require at some point in their education.

It is also the case that he did need an extra year in kindergarten to handle the demands. However, this decision is not at all uncommon for children who are enrolled in school at age four.

Mrs. Love's declaration contains other information that contradicts a diagnosis of ADHD—Combined Type. She indicated that he was "shy and timid" through his early formative years and that he was "never a discipline problem" in school. She also described him as a "hard worker and dedicated student." To say the least, these are not characterizations applied to youngsters who meet diagnostic criteria for the disorder. By definition, they are impulsive and thrill-seeking children who routinely have discipline problems and find it difficult to dedicate themselves to work.

Mrs. Love's declaration also provides evidence that whatever problems her son may have experienced taking standardized tests could easily be attributable to test anxiety rather than a formal psychiatric or learning disorder. Whenever he took such tests "he felt he was under a lot of pressure and would become very stressed and anxious." Even on practice tests he would "get anxious and have trouble concentrating" to the point that he would "shut down." These are clearly the reactions of an individual whose test anxiety can interfere to some extent with performance.

The test-taking problems of individuals with ADHD rarely surface because of test anxiety, per se. As a group, they perform poorly on tests because they are impulsive, inattentive, and disorganized. In fact, most report that they are so restless and poor at gauging the adequacy of their performance that they do not fully use the time allotted to take the test.

With the declaration submitted to the Court, I was now ready to be deposed. After the predictable negotiations around time and place, it was scheduled for 8 AM on September 7, in Syracuse. All parties agreed to hold the deposition in a conference room within my department. It was comforting to know I would be questioned in familiar surroundings, in fact, a room in which I regularly attended meetings and lectured.

A surprise participant in the proceedings was the lawyer who came to Syracuse to depose me. Ms. JoAnne Simon is a Brooklyn-based attorney well known for her work in the accommodations arena. She specializes in helping post-secondary students who have been denied accommodations on standardized testing. Many of us involved in documentation reviews have seen the forceful letters she writes to testing organizations on behalf of her clients.

Ms. Simon's enduring claim to fame is that she successfully represented Marilyn J. Bartlett in her lawsuit against the State of New York. The ruling in this case, one that Judge Surrick refers to in his opinion (see Chapter 7), stands as a singular instance in which a court concurred with the notion that someone can be high achieving, yet still legally disabled. Dr. Bartlett was indeed an accomplished learner. Despite her purported dyslexia, she earned a bachelor's degree in Early Childhood Education from State College at Worcester, a master's degree in Special Education from Boston University, a Ph.D. in Organizational and Administrative Studies from New York University, and her J.D. from Vermont Law School. Her work history, detailed in her biography on the University of South Florida Web site where she now teaches, reflects a high level of functioning. Nonetheless, she won the right to extended time and other accommodations after having failed the New York State bar examination five times.

Why the plaintiff's attorneys sent Ms. Simon to conduct my deposition is unclear. It may have been a matter of logistics, given that her offices were closer to mine than were those of the California-based DRA. However, if it were simply a matter of practicalities and economics, I would imagine that they would have been content if they were represented by Mr. Charles Weiner, the lawyer who filed the initial motion in this lawsuit. His offices, located in Bucks County, Pennsylvania, are a four-hour car trip from Syracuse. While he may have been first hired because he was located in the appropriate jurisdiction for a lawsuit against the Pennsylvania-based LSAC (and therefore a suitable "local counsel"), he was certainly familiar with the case, had an ongoing involvement, and specialized in disability law.

Another possibility for Ms. Simon's arrival in Central New York may have been that she had deposed me before. In 1999, I was involved in the case of *Rebecca W. Root v. Georgia State Board of Veterinary Medicine*. Ms. Simon was one of the lawyers who argued the case for the plaintiff. After receiving her undergraduate degree, Ms. Root taught middle school in Georgia. While working full time, she earned a master's degree in education and, several years later, a master's degree in community counseling. In 1993, Ms. Root was admitted to the University of Georgia Veterinary School, from which she graduated in 1996. Of the three tests veterinarians in Georgia have to pass in order to practice, Ms. Root was successful on two of them, but failed a four-hundred-item National Board Exam on eight attempts. After several failures, she requested test accommodations, even though a prior evaluation determined that she did not have a learning disability. However, after a counselor at the Regents' Center for Learning Disorders at the University of Georgia determined that she had test anxiety, Ms. Root applied and was granted the accommodations of extra time and an individual testing room (even though test anxiety is not a psychiatric condition). Unfortunately, she still failed the exam. Ms. Root now returned to the Regents' center for a re-evaluation, which declared that she actually suffered from a learning disability and ADHD. With those diagnoses in hand, she requested additional accommodations, most notably someone to read the questions to her. After having failed the test under these conditions, she complained that the reader was not sufficiently well-versed in veterinary jargon. After still not passing the test with a more suitable reader, Ms. Root sued the Board of Veterinary Medicine.

As the reader might imagine, I expressed some skepticism in my deposition testimony with Ms. Simon that someone with Ms. Root's resume could fairly be considered substantially impaired because of deficits in learning and attention. It seemed unlikely to me that someone with two master's degrees and a doctorate in veterinary medicine was limited when compared to most people, given that most people do not even earn a four-year college degree. The case was eventually thrown out, more on a technicality than after a ruling focused on ADA-issues.

My deposition for the Love case lasted three hours and eighteen minutes, including one break of about a half hour. In attendance were Ms. Simon, Mr. Wiener, a court reporter, and Ms. Grace Deon, a co-counsel for the LSAC defense team. Ms. Simon and I did almost all the talking, with occasional "objections as to the form of the question" by Ms. Deon. In that no judge was in attendance, I imagine these objections, usually to a question that was vague or wordy, were to establish grounds for having my answer thrown out at trial should it become an issue. In other depositions, it was clear that these objections were sometimes raised to irritate the opposing counsel. No such dynamic played itself out in our third-floor conference room that day. The tone all around was civil, the atmosphere task oriented.

Much to my embarrassment, Ms. Deon also had to tell me several times to let Ms. Simon finish her questions before I answered them. Despite the concerted efforts of many fine lawyers over the years to prepare me for deposition hearings, I still jumped in abruptly and lectured too much. Adopting the role of educator in such a proceeding does have its downsides.

Ms. Simon first asked me about the nature of my relationship with the LSAC and the procedures for submitting a documentation review. She inquired how many reviews I wrote for them, the average amount of time I billed for each review, and any instructions I received from the LSAC on how to prepare my report. She also asked how I received the documentation and what information I had reviewed in preparing the Love report. Her questions probed whether I had any conflicts of interest or undue influence on the outcome of the LSAC's decisions regarding accommodations.

I testified about how I came to receive the documentation and submit my report. I made clear in response to her questions that I was not the one who decided on whether or not an applicant was granted accommodations. My role was to offer an opinion to the administrators responsible for making that decision. Indeed, I am not privy to the organization's decision on an accommodations request unless an applicant appeals a denial.

Other questions about the administrative process were geared toward determining whether the LSAC in any way tried to influence my recommendation about accommodations. Ms. Simon asked if anyone from the testing organization called me during the time I was preparing my documentation review. I indicated that I did not remember having any contact with Ms. Dempsey (the LSAC administrator in charge of accommodated testing) around the Love case; if we had communicated, it was to make sure I had all the information that Love had submitted or perhaps that I was aware how quickly she needed my report. I made the point that consultants get paid the same amount regardless of whether they check "approve" or "deny." I also have indicated that, in my experience, testing organizations are not looking for reasons to reject an application. I would not work for an organization that seemed bent on denying accommodations requests even for those individuals with legitimate disabilities. The goal is to maintain integrity and fairness in the process, not to discriminate against people with legitimate claims.

Most of the deposition addressed the review I submitted to the LSAC about Mr. Love's application. Ms. Simon had me detail and justify the guidelines I used to arrive at my recommendations. We first discussed the criterion regarding the age by which symptoms must cause impairment. Because I acknowledged that the DSM-IV's requirement that problems had to surface before age seven was overly restrictive, the two of us had little to debate on that score.

We spent more time skirmishing around what constituted substantial impairment, the issue that sat squarely at the heart of this case. She worked hard to get me to come across as a nonbeliever in the legitimacy of ADHD in adults and as someone with an aberrant view of what constituted impairment. For reasons that became clear at trial, she tried to establish that Mr. Love's average LSAT score was pivotal in my recommendation:

Q. So, the fact that it's [his LSAT score] in the average range is in your mind preclusive of his having attention deficit disorder?

A. In my mind the fact that he was in the average range indicated that, whether he had ADHD or not, he was able to take a test at least as well as most people, if not better.

Q. So, you're – the fact that he was able to score in the average range does not indicate in your mind that he doesn't have ADHD, it only indicates that he could take a test and score in the average range?

A. The most, the most significant aspect of it is that he could take a test most people wouldn't even be in a position to take and get an average score. It would be hard for me to conjure a circumstance in which somebody who was disabled by ADHD even got to the point of being able to take the test. And so it does impact my sense of whether ADHD makes sense [as a diagnosis for Mr. Love]. But again, I'm looking at the extent to which he's functionally impaired … does his diagnosis limit his ability to take a test? And I think one has to look at that [LSAT score] and say, well, no.

Q. So, in your mind essentially functional impairment is indicated by below the average range scores on a timed test?

A. Functional impairment as it relates to testing would surface first whether the person even was capable enough to get to the position of taking a test to get into law school …

My goal in this interchange (but also more generally) was to keep the focus on the extent to which Mr. Love was actually impaired relative to other people. As I see it, what counts is evidence of poor functioning, not examples of sub-stellar performance on complicated examinations. An average score on a professional entrance exam alone is not a symptom of a psychiatric disorder. Also, I wanted to have on the record that Jonathan Love's average LSAT score, while not solely determinative of my opinion, did serve as a marker for his overall high level of functioning.

A similar discussion ensued when Ms. Simon questioned me about these two sentences in my declaration (again, derived from the original documentation review): "Indeed, his score in the 46th percentile on your test is solidly average. He therefore clearly and demonstrably has the neuropsychological capacity to take a timed examination at least as well as most people." Ms. Simon began this line of questioning as follows:

Q. Now, I'm going to move to paragraph where you talk about what is most relevant to your current determination is the fact that Mr. Love has taken high stakes tests under timed conditions and scored within the average range. And you state in the last sentence of that paragraph that he has the neuropsychological capacity to take a timed examination at least as well as most people. Is it your testimony that in order to have attention deficit disorder one cannot have the neuropsychological capacity to take an exam and score at least as well as most people?

A. My comment in paragraph fourteen is directed towards the idea that whatever is going on for Mr. Love, whether it's ADHD related or not ADHD related, or related to any other aspect of his functioning, he has the capacity to take a test at least as well as most people. So, in a way, when I'm making that statement, I'm saying ADHD, no ADHD, reading problems, no reading problems, he was able to function as well as most people in his capacity to do that [take a test].

Q. Okay. And is it your opinion that his functional ability, that functioning is indicated by a score on a test, that that's in fact an evaluation of functioning . . .

A. My testimony is that given his performance on all these tests, not just the LSAT but all the tests that he has taken, he shows evidence of being able to manage a timed, standardized, high stakes test.

Q. And what do you mean by "manage"?

A. To perform at least as well as most people who would take that test which, incidentally, is a refined group.

The ensuing interchange reflected the plaintiff's stance that, even though he had an average score on the LSAT, his score could have been higher:

Q. By "manage," do you mean that he's actually read all the questions?

A. He's able to do whatever is necessary to be able to get to the test, handle the test in a way that he could do at least as well as most of the other people taking the test.

Q. Okay. Let me rephrase – restate my question. Which is: Do you assume that by managing the test that one has actually read all the questions?

A. Well, in many of these tests there are more questions than one could answer.

Q. I'm talking about the—let's stick with the LSAT.

A. I don't know if he read every answer or not . . . he read enough to be able to get an average score. That's my assumption.

Q. Okay.

A. Whether he read every single one of them I couldn't know.

Ms. Simon asked me to consider other signs that might indicate Mr. Love was impaired. In particular, she asked me if someone who had been tutored "every day of every week of every year" would qualify as impaired. I responded that tutoring was common for many students; witness the popularity of the services offered by companies such as Huntington Learning Centers or Sylvan Learning Centers. She also alluded to information from teachers that indicated he was indeed impaired during childhood. I simply responded that I could only review what he submitted; no such information was included in the documentation.

Another exchange addressed whether I dismissed the possibility that any-one with ADHD could get into law school:

Q. Is it your belief that the fact that [if] somebody progresses through col-lege, that that is preclusive of having attention deficit disorder?

A. That is not my position.

Q. Okay. How do you reconcile the fact that that is not your position with your sense that this is so rare that somebody would get through college and –

A. It's not incompatible. It's possible [for someone with ADHD to gain admission to law school]. I never said it was impossible nor have I ever written as such. I have just indicated that statistically it's going to be unlikely given all the things we've discussed. There are individuals who, despite very significant impairment and with accommodations that soar beyond just getting some informal extra time from professors, are some-how able to make it – much to everybody's delight and sometimes sur-prise. Usually they've received wholesale and very substantial help both academically and otherwise. So, it is possible … So, the answer to your question, "Do I think that it's possible for somebody that had ADHD to go onto higher education?" is, yes I've seen it, I believe it, I just don't think it's a very common event.

The deposition moved on to cover topics that recurred often during the following months of depositions, preparations, and trial. The first addressed the extent to which psychological testing could be relied upon to diagnose ADHD, a matter that becomes more central later in the process:

Q. Okay. Now, earlier you talked about the criteria that you use, what you look for in a report and following of the DSM-IV criteria. One of the things you didn't talk about was the psychoeducational testing or psy-chometric testing. To what extent do you believe that such testing needs to be given or administered in the assessment of somebody to determine that they have an attention deficit disorder? And I'm not talking about the possible comorbidity, et cetera,

A. I need to disclose something first.

Q. Mm-hm, sure.

A. I'm the developer of one of the tests commonly administered…

Q. I know.

A. …as part of an ADHD diagnosis and my response should be judged accordingly. And now having made that clear, the diagnosis of ADHD rides predominantly on clinical history and evidence of current impairment…

Q. Mm-hm.

A. …and any clinician, even one who has developed a test used for the di-agnosis of ADHD, needs to amass data from actual functioning that somebody is clinically and significantly impaired. … Unfortunately, and

much to my own economic disadvantage, these tests are not as useful in
people over the age of twelve to fourteen. There's very little research on
them [for adults]. So, for an individual who is college aged, while the
testing may be corroborative, it would be considered wholly inappropriate to diagnose somebody based on that testing. I don't know any person, you know, clinical researcher in this area, me included, who would
suggest that [reliance on psychological tests for diagnosis].

We covered other potential signs of disability. After having me acknowledge that not everyone with ADHD has a history of grade retention and
placement in special education, she asked how me how much weight I would
give to a family history of the disorder. I responded that, based on scientific
data, a documented family history might increase the odds of an individual
having ADHD, but not enough to make that factor diagnostically significant.

The deposition concluded around noon without bursting fireworks or
surprises. I was relieved that Ms. Deon did not find it necessary to ask me
questions when Ms. Simon had finished with me. I assumed that meant I
managed not to say anything so damaging as to require clarification. Reasonably confident that I had justified my position well, I was nonetheless
aware that the worst was yet to come.

The hardest part of any deposition, for me, occurs the following week
when the transcript arrives for corrections. Having left the deposition convinced I had presented my arguments with precision and a masterful use of
language, I confront the painful reality of the court reporter's transcript. By
about page ten I begin to wonder whether I had suffered a trans ischemic
attack or two that rendered me confused, inarticulate, and disorganized. By
the twentieth page I marvel that the plaintiff's attorney withheld the urge to
request of the defense counsel that the witness be removed from the case
and placed in an "English as a second language" course. I rarely make it past
page thirty without considering a change of careers, perhaps to one that
requires little, if any, verbal communication. I have learned to cope by reading the depositions of other expert witnesses, most of which fall similarly
(and mercifully) short of perfection.

More interesting than testifying at my own deposition was helping the
LSAC lawyers prepare for their encounters with the opposing witnesses. I
was assigned to help them depose Drs. AliceAnne Brunn, M. Kay Runyan,
and Hugh Van Auken. After reading their declarations, clinical reports, and
protocols, I generated lists of questions that Ms. Leopold-Leventhal and
Ms. Deon might choose to ask. I also wrote documents intended to brief the
lawyers on topics that, in my opinion, were important for them to understand prior to facing these clinicians. Of all the phases of this trial, I most

enjoyed this one because it offered me the opportunity to think critically, research topics I had not examined as carefully in the past, and teach unusually bright and eager "students"—all at a handsome hourly fee. Perfect.

For the record, the LSAC lawyers were selective in which of my questions they used in the depositions. Lawyers have to be judicious about what they ask in depositions. As I mentioned earlier, they want to avoid giving the opposing attorneys an opportunity to develop a counterstrategy for use at trial. Even some of Ms. Simon's questions to me sent us to the Internet and library to gather data about issues she raised, for example, the number of children enrolled in private tutoring services and how special education laws applied to private schools during the early 1990s.

While my catalogs of questions for these depositions (and, eventually, cross-examination at trial) addressed every possible angle I could imagine, most followed a similar logic. I thought that the first step was to have experts identify the criteria for ADHD. In this way they would have to declare the centrality of identifying evidence of early onset, pervasiveness, chronicity, and clinically significant impairment associated with ADHD symptoms. They would then have to justify their assignment of that diagnosis given Jonathan Love's record of competence in academic, social, and employment settings.

The second step was to have witnesses articulate their understanding of what qualifies an individual as disabled under the ADA. As indicated by our 2002 survey (see Chapter 3, p. 10), most clinicians misconstrue the intent of the ADA; they regard it as designed to ensure that an individual performs up to his or her presumed potential. By having the witness articulate that (errant) position, attorneys can help the judge can see that the expert's opinion was based on an incorrect reading of the law.

Such was the situation in a precedent-setting case from 1997 in Huntington, West Virginia. In *Price v. National Board of Medical Examiners*, three Marshall University School of Medicine students sought extra time and a separate room in which to take the United States Medical Licensing Examination (USMLE) board examination. All three had been diagnosed by the National Center of Higher Education for Learning Problems (HELP) with ADHD and/or learning disabilities. These students were unusually high-achieving. I happened to have performed the documentation review for one of the students, Brian Singleton. He was in a gifted program from second grade through high school, from which he graduated with a 4.2 (out of 4) grade point average. Among other accomplishments, he was the state debate champion in high school, graduated from Vanderbilt University with a major in physics, and gained admission to the US Naval Academy.

According to my now-yellowed notes, he sought extra time when he received a B minus grade on a neurochemistry exam in medical school. He felt something must have been wrong with him given that he failed to get a higher grade.

Aside from the realities of these students' academic prowess, Judge Godwin noted both in the courtroom and in his opinion that the clinicians from HELP had it wrong when it came to the ADA. To quote from the decision:

> Plaintiffs' three experts misapprehend the meaning of "disability" within the ADA. Two of the professionals at HELP, and an additional expert testifying on behalf of the plaintiffs, testified to their belief that a person who is not performing up to his or her abilities has a disability within the meaning of the ADA. Dr. Barbara Guyer testified, "The law says that you must look at the discrepancies between their ability and their achievement." Deborah Painter testified that "the problem that we have with the Board's decision was that they're saying that if an individual's processing is average, there is no problem." Dr. MacCallum gave his opinion in response to a question from plaintiffs' attorney: "Q. The bottom line is what you're saying is that the issue is whether a person can function at the level that person is capable of functioning at. That's your standard, true? A. That's correct."

The judge affirmed that an individual is disabled under the ADA when he has an impairment which substantially limits a major life activity "in comparison with most people." Perceived underachievement was not a basis for qualifying an individual as disabled.

Having established the witness's understanding of diagnostic and legal criteria, the attorneys in my personal courtroom scenario would now lay out the facts of Jonathan Love's life. They ask if the expert is aware of Mr. Love's benign early history, solid academic achievement, graduation from Baylor University, enrollment in an MBA program at Notre Dame, and so forth. As the evidence unfolds, the lawyers keep asking questions like, "Doctor, you told me that the DSM requires onset early in childhood but you acknowledge that Mr. Love was never retained, never identified as in need of special education, never in any situation that would seem to reflect abnormal adjustment. How can you square the early onset criterion with all this evidence of a normal early childhood?" Or, "You indicated in your report that, to meet criteria for ADHD, a person has to show 'clinically significant impairment.' But you acknowledge that he received his bachelor's degree from a major university without requiring any formal accommodations. How can you reconcile those two positions?"

Confronted with these inconsistencies, the expert has little option but to veer from the tenets of the ADA, the requirements of the DSM, and/or the facts of Jonathan Love's life. And, in their real-life depositions and subsequent testimony, the plaintiff's experts traveled down all three paths. The most common strategy was to presume that the ADA covered individuals who functioned well, but had the potential to function even better. They also played fast and loose with the DSM by fabricating ADHD subtypes or selectively ignoring certain criteria. And, without question, they fully embraced the "sour cherry picking" gambit for reviewing clinical data whereby every minor deviation from excellence is deemed indicative of major disability. An expert has other options, such as ignoring information about competent daily functioning by over-focusing on scores from psychological testing.

Presented below in its entirety is an example of a note that I prepared prior to the deposition of Dr. Brunn, a psychologist who evaluated Mr. Love in 2004. It derived from my review of the report she submitted on behalf of Mr. Love. The Life History Questionnaire I refer to was a form that Dr. Brunn had Mr. Love complete. The IVA is a computerized test of attention that Dr. Brunn administered:

> Dr. Bunn's report contains a host of statements that are hard to justify based either on the information she had at hand or on facts that have surfaced over time. Indeed, she was remarkably unconcerned about some obvious disconnects between the clinical data she had gathered and the conclusions she drew, especially as they related to his actual functioning at the time of the evaluation. I get the impression that she was intent on identifying him as disabled from the outset and chose to ignore any bits of information that might interfere with that process.
>
> Dr. Bunn's findings seem to evolve from the notion that someone should be considered disabled if either one of the two following conditions pertains:
>
> • The individual considers himself able to perform better than he has performed, even if he hasn't performed all that poorly in the past; and
> • One can identify isolated scores from psychological testing that are low relative to certain cherry-picked IQ indices, even though those low scores have never been tied empirically to impairment in actual functioning.
>
> From Dr. Bunn's point of view, if you have to choose between test scores and reality, you go with test scores. For example, she was surprised he's done as well as he's done on standardized testing given some of his scores on psych testing. Of course, one could also question the validity of those tests for predicting performance on standardized examinations like the LSAT – but she doesn't consider that possibility. From her point of view, information about actual functioning pales in diagnostic significance to the scores she generates on psychological testing.

Her testimony may provide the opportunity to focus on certain specific issues relative to Mr. Love's then current functioning that pertain to his qualification as being disabled. Although she writes in her conclusion that Mr. Love manifests a substantial limitation that affects his "day to day functioning at home and in school," she had information at the time that would directly discount that conclusion. Getting her to acknowledge that information would support the claim that his evaluators failed to grasp what ADA requires to qualify someone as impaired and that they mischaracterized the extent to which he was maladjusted. Specifically:

- On the Life History Questionnaire (page 9), Mr. Love specifically reported that he had no problems managing the demands for organization inherent in daily life. He indicated that he could drive, clean the house, do laundry, prepare meals, keep a checkbook, and shop for groceries and household items. He acknowledges in those responses that he is unimpaired in his ability to handle routine demands. Individuals with ADHD, by definition and regardless of how bright they are, run into their most serious problems handling exactly these kinds of routine demands for attention and organization. His responses (especially given everything else we know about him) rule out the kind of global impairment required by the criteria for the diagnosis of ADHD. They directly contradict her statement that he is substantially impaired in his ability to function in a home environment. The only way she can respond is to indicate that he is a "high-functioning ADHD individual" whose problems are circumscribed to taking high-stakes examinations. Of course, that gives you all kinds of ammunition to shoot down the notion that he is truly impaired in a major life activity. It also allows you to get her to show her ignorance about ADA requirements for qualifying someone as disabled.

- Dr. Brunn reports that she contacted Mr. Love's academic adviser, Roseanne Fuller. Ms. Fuller described her advisee as an "extremely diligent student" who was receiving good grades in a difficult course of study. She saw no basis for referring him for services and was unaware of any accommodations he might have been receiving (perhaps because he wasn't actually using them much, if at all). To say the least, students with ADHD are described as anything but "extremely diligent." In many ways, it's a disorder of diligence, of task persistence. Saying that someone with ADHD can be extremely diligent is like saying that a blind person can see especially well. The comments by Ms. Fuller in concert with the information that he was a good student in a four year university stand in stark contrast to her statement that his purported ADHD substantially limits his academic functioning. Was he limited because he could have had a 3.8 average? Is that a disability? By the way, on the Life History Form, he indicates that his reading, writing, and math were all "good." Again, the only thing that apparently wasn't good was his comfort level around the LSAT score.

Several other points:

- Dr. Brunn only tested him off his medication. While that might be justified if one were only interested in judging someone's functioning untreated, it's not appropriate for an ADA-related exam where, as you well know, the issue is how well someone functions with (or without) mitigating measures. Even if Mr. Love were ADHD, it still would have to be determined that he couldn't function normally with his medication or informal accommodations. You can't do that if you don't see someone also on their meds. It would be interesting to question Dr. Brunn about her decision, as a way of demonstrating her lack of sophistication about ADA and her obvious desire to portray Mr. Love at his worst so she could justify a recommendation that he be granted accommodations.

- Dr. Brunn makes much of Mr. Love's performance on a computerized psychological test, the IVA. As we've discussed, I wouldn't recommend getting much into the nuances of his test scores; I think it would be better to focus her on his actual functioning, not his performance on these measures. But you should know that absolutely no data exist from independent, peer-reviewed studies to support the validity of its interpretive reports for college-aged students. In fact, it's not entirely clear whether there are even norms for this age cohort. In one independent study of the measure with children, the false positive rate was 36 percent. Based on data from other such measures used with adults (including one I developed), it's probably at least as high if not higher in adults. No justification exists for using this measure alone to diagnose an individual with ADHD. To claim someone has ADHD-type impairment based on scores from this test, especially when ample evidence exists that Mr. Love has a life history reflective of overall competence, is out of bounds. So if she says he has ADHD because the IVA scores were abnormal, you can ask, "Are the IVA scores so predictive of performance on a timed examination that they can trump real-life information that he achieves scores in the average range on such exams?" "You'd believe a test for which no published data exist for adult populations over hard core evidence of test-taking competence?"

- Although I know you're focusing on ADHD and not learning disorders (because Mr. Love didn't self-identify learning problems when he applied for accommodations), you perhaps should still be aware that the disorders Dr. Brunn identified ("Disorders of Academic Fluency and Processing Speed") are not disorders in any formal or validated sense of the term. In other words, if you look in the DSM-IV, you won't find Academic Fluency or Processing Speed disorders listed. She made them up (as clinicians are apt to do) based on certain clusters of psychological test scores that were relatively lower than others. It's based on the idea that: 1) someone with a low scores on the Processing Speed Index of the intelligence test (for example) will, in real life, process information slowly; and 2) low scores on that index can only be due to neuropsychological problems tied directly to how quickly the brain processes information. The reality is that no evidence exists to support either contention. It is not at all clear that the index is tied to how quickly someone reads, performs academic or occupational tasks, etc. And it's definitely unclear what it means when someone does poorly on this index because it can be low in people with psychiatric problems (such as anxiety and depression), learning problems, or no problems at all.

- As with Dr. Van Auken, Dr. Brunn takes the mother's report regarding early impairment at face value, without any consideration that Ms. Love might have been advocating for her son rather than presenting information objectively when she described him as extremely hyperactive as a child. Dr. Brunn doesn't also consider that the distractibility the mother described could be due to issues other than those related to ADHD, for example anxiety, avoidance, and boredom. I imagine one could have a field day asking Dr. Brunn questions like, "Were you aware that Mr. Love's mother responded to the question, 'What was most difficult about raising your child' with the response, 'Nothing. He was a blessing and a very good child?' Does that sound like he was hyperactive and impulsive to you? If Mr. Love were so disruptive, why did she put him in school at age 4? Why didn't she ever consult her pediatrician? Why in the world wouldn't a parent take her highly dysregulated child to a psychiatrist or psychologist? If you had an extremely distractible, impaired child, wouldn't you take him or her for a consultation with a professional?

- Much of the questioning of Dr. Brunn could touch on the same issues I outlined in response to Dr. Van Auken's file. Specifically:

  - Pushing the witness to acknowledge that Love's done well for himself from childhood onward regardless of what her tests say.

  - Exposing her ignorance of the distinction between clinical diagnosis and legal determination. You can ask those same questions about what ADA requires for a qualification of disability, etc. What I think you'll find is that she disagrees with the Supreme Court, and proudly so.

  - Targeting her credibility as an objective evaluator by pointing out that she ignored evidence that directly contradicted her conclusions. One might also ask her diagnostic habits either in private practice or when she worked for Baylor. How many students has she evaluated for ADHD as part of an effort to secure accommodations? Of that number, how many did not meet her criteria for ADHD? Could she describe a scenario of someone who sought an ADHD diagnosis but didn't get one? How was that person different that Mr. Love?

The depositions of the three witnesses followed roughly the blueprint I had conjured in my mind. The deposition of Dr. Brunn adhered to the scenario most closely. Her testimony offered ample fodder for cannon shots at trial. Without subjecting the reader to a full analysis of the sort I prepared for the lawyers post-deposition, here are some highlights:

- Dr. Brunn acknowledged many of the points the defense expert witnesses had made in depositions. These include that: early symptom onset must be present; impairment must be in two or more settings; teachers' contemporaneous reports are worthwhile; the need for tutoring is not limited to individuals with ADHD; Mr. Love is a high-functioning individual who had no problems managing routine daily activities; his mother never had him evaluated because tutoring was sufficient in helping him achieve at an expected level; and most people would do better on the LSAT if they were given extra time.

- The testimony made it clear that Dr. Brunn had no familiarity with what the ADA requires by way of impairment. When asked, "Do you understand there to be a difference between a clinical definition of impairment and a legal definition of impairment?" she responded, "I'm not familiar with that. You might want to describe it more to me, because that's not something I'm very familiar with. No, I'm not familiar with legal definitions of things in general, because I don't do forensic work."

- Dr. Brunn's method of determining a diagnosis was, as predicted, one that many clinicians rely upon, that is, relative discrepancies between certain test scores and the overall IQ. She testified, "Generally the criterion I use is the degree of difference between the performance in the problem area – in Jonathan's case it would be his processing speed – and the ability level. So if a student had two standard deviations difference, I recommend twice the time."

- From Dr. Brunn's perspective, if the patient feels he has a problem, he has a problem. In her words, "The client determines when he is having difficulty." She elaborated as follows: "In terms of how severe the difficulty has to be, in my training I was taught that when a problem disturbs the client or someone close to the client, then it's severe enough to warrant attention clinically."

- Dr. Brunn presented notions about ADHD that were, in my opinion, difficult to justify empirically. We made note of them in preparation for trial, including the commonly-held but errant idea that individuals with ADHD could be hypervigilant. Among other things, she also suggested that someone with ADHD can perform normally on a particular test because the symptoms happened not to affect him that day.

The component of Dr. Brunn's testimony that was most central to this case concerned the criteria she used to judge the presence of a disorder. She stated unequivocally that a student should be identified as having a disorder when it "creates difficulties for them in achieving goals they want to achieve. For example, in Jonathan's case, why wasn't he performing as well on the LSAT as he had hoped to perform?" That statement perfectly reflects the thought process of many clinicians, not to mention the theory behind the plaintiff's filing of the lawsuit.

Of the many junctures at which I (wrongly) thought that Mr. Love and his attorneys would drop their case, none seemed more decisive than after the deposition of Dr. Hugh Van Auken, the clinician who had most recently evaluated the plaintiff. In his declaration, Dr. Van Auken traveled the same ground as his predecessors, accepting at face value Mr. Love's statements that he had trouble reading and concentrating as a child and that he had to work much harder than others to achieve. The clinician also relied on the psychological testing that he and Dr. Brunn had administered.

In the face of persistent and detailed questioning from Ms. Leopold-Leventhal, Dr. Van Auken conceded repeatedly that Mr. Love appeared to have been an able student who was also competent in managing non-academic aspects of his life. At no point was Dr. Van Auken able to identify evidence of poor functioning because of ADHD or learning problems. Nonetheless, he doggedly held onto his clinical diagnoses because the realities of Mr. Love's actual functioning were secondary in his mind to the import of certain psychological test scores that he and Dr. Brunn had gathered. When asked how Mr. Love could have a reading disorder given his fine performance on a string of high-stakes tests, he responded:

> Diagnostic tests can reveal things that placement tests can't reveal or may not necessarily reveal. If an individual does poorly on diagnostic tests, that suggests the presence of a disability of one type or another. These types of tests that are taken for placement issues, SAT, LSAT, ACT, are not diagnostic tests. They're tests that are used for placement issues.

In other words, reality be damned, my tests know all. He held to this position, even admitting along the way that the results of one measure, the Nelson-Denny Reading Test, likely represented an underestimate of Jonathan Love's reading abilities.

To Dr. Van Auken's substantial credit, he did have a sense that the legal definition of ADHD could differ from the criteria that clinicians used in their practice:

Q. What is your understanding of a disability?
A. My understanding ... is that a disability must be substantially limiting relative to the average person. Clinically, the standard is that an individual must show some impairment; although, in certain components it isn't relative to the average person. For example, a discrepancy analysis for disabilities, learning disabilities evaluations looks at impairment as an issue, but not necessarily stressing the substantial limitation relative to the average person component.

With that awareness of the ADA standard, Dr. Van Auken made a concession that, to my mind, would send us all packing. He admitted in response to several questions from Ms. Leopold-Leventhal, that Mr. Love may well not be impaired in his test-taking:

Q. Okay. Would you agree with me that, assuming your diagnosis is correct, the LD and the ADHD, that with an average LSAT score Mr. Love is not substantially impaired in taking the LSAT?
A. If he obtains an average score, I would have to say that there isn't sufficient evidence to say that he is impaired on taking the LSAT ... Again, if you will look at the data, his scores have all been within normal limits on an unaccommodated test. It's then a difficult argument to make that he should receive accommodations.

To my mind, that admission from the clinician who submitted to the LSAC the form that supposedly verified a disability was a stab in the heart of the plaintiff's case. How could they continue with their legal action? Their main expert witness just acknowledged in sworn testimony that Mr. Love was not legally disabled. He squarely articulated the position the defense had adopted all along. Game over, right? Wrong again.

Near the end of the deposition, Ms. Leopold-Leventhal asked a series of questions that seemed designed to discount the argument that someone was disabled if his LSAT scores were in the average range but his IQ scores were in the above average range. The notion that a disability is defined by a discrepancy between intelligence and achievement was at the core of the argument all three plaintiff's experts made to bolster their contention that Jonathan Love should get accommodations.

The first set of questions appeared aimed at establishing the absurdity of justifying accommodations on the presumption that any test score that fell in a range below a person's IQ was a sign of disability. She clearly wanted Dr. Van Auken to acknowledge that IQ was not a perfect predictor of "potential" on the LSAT. If it were, why not just give extra time to every applicant whose scores were lower than the level one might supposedly predict from the IQ score? Better yet, why not make admission to law school contingent on one's IQ?

> Q. After looking at various barometers, as well as Mr. Love's IQ score, verbal and full, you concluded that he needs extra time, "... in testing in order for Mr. Love to demonstrate his true ability." Would you agree with me that the student's need or right to extended time isn't based on their demonstration of their disability, but rather a finding of an impairment and the impact of that impairment?
> A. So, essentially, the distinction that's being made is between impairment versus disability?
> Q. No. I'm asking you whether or not your focus was on his demonstration of his potential, or your finding of an impairment and the impact of that impairment.
> A. It would be the second of the two choices ...
> Q. So, in your understanding, there's no study that is able to predict or correlate a person's IQ score with their performance on the LSAT?
> A. Not that I'm aware of.
> Q. And there's nothing, in your understanding, professionally, that would provide some sort of one-to-one correlation that, if this is your IQ score, this is what you'll get on the LSAT, correct?
> A. I'm not aware of that.
> Q. And if that were the case, people would just walk in to their law school and hand them their IQ score and not need to take the LSAT.
> A. I'm a 128; let me into law school.
> Q. Right.
> A. That's illegal.

Another element of the attack on the "IQ as predictor of potential" argument came to mind when I was preparing for my own deposition. It dawned on me that, while IQ was moderately tied to educational outcome, so too was socioeconomic status. Indeed, the correlations were in the same general range. Given that wealthier people had the "potential" for higher achievement, should we not give accommodations to rich students with low test scores? Would Dr. Van Auken advocate extra time based on someone's financial resources? Apparently not:

> Q. Are you aware also of a correlation, similar to the correlation between IQ and LSAT, between socioeconomic status and LSAT score?
> A. Yes. Socioeconomic status is a very good predictor of performance on the SAT and other tests of that ilk.

Q. Should a person receive higher accommodations on the LSAT to allow them to achieve their predicted score based on this socioeconomic level?

A. Should a person receive accommodations for this economic level?

Q. To achieve a score that would be predicted by their socioeconomic level.

A. Hypothetically, socioeconomic status should not play a role in the determination whether somebody receives accommodations.

One last reaction to Dr. Van Auken's deposition: In an apparent effort to boost my stock with the judge, Ms. Leopold-Leventhal asked him if he had heard of me. He responded that he indeed knew of my work, particularly the book I edited (with Ms. Shelby Keiser) on accommodations in higher education. He then uttered words that could inspire a poem entitled, "The Professor's Lament." Dr. Van Auken testified, "Much of my understanding of ADA comes from his understanding in that text."

Well, that book, especially the chapter on ADHD that I wrote along with my colleague, Dr. Kevin Murphy, was intended to discourage clinicians from following the precise course that Dr. Van Auken pursued in supporting accommodations for Jonathan Love. We advised clinicians in stark terms to gather information in addition to self-report, to avoid overreliance on test scores, and to build a case that the individual was impaired relative to most people.

What happened? How could someone as obviously bright and capable as Dr. Van Auken read that book and still submit a verification of disability for Jonathan Love? Why do workshop presenters despair when they read notes about their seminar an attendee posted on the Web? How could people so grossly misinterpret major points you thought you had presented with pristine clarity and force? Social psychologists would respond with the two words: confirmation bias. We humans tend to judge information in terms of how it supports our preconceptions, not as a basis for adopting new ideas, much to the dismay of teachers everywhere. Ah well.

CHAPTER 5

A Cautionary Tale

At the outset, the case of *Love* v. *LSAC* was all about diagnostic guidelines, legal standards, and the life of Jonathan M. Love. The guiding theory underlying an effective defense was easily gleaned: the Americans with Disabilities Act requires evidence of abnormal functioning relative to most people; Mr. Love functions at least as well as most people, end of story. The defense simply had to amass as much ammunition as possible to discredit the idea that he was substantially impaired.

As transcripts, graduate school applications, medical documentation, report cards, and other records began to arrive at the law offices of Eastburn & Gray, those plans appeared to become subject to revision. Signs of a change in strategy were evident in e-mails from the lead counsel for the defense, Ms. Leopold-Leventhal. They often began with a sentence like, "You won't believe what I just found out." Ms. Leopold-Leventhal would then describe evidence she had received that highlighted significant discrepancies between the Love family account and what emerged from other sources.

Those discrepancies began to pile higher and higher as weeks passed, to such an extent that the lawyers told me that they were contemplating making credibility an issue. From what I could gather of their position, the judge had to know the extent to which Mr. Love and his mother had tailored the truth to help them achieve their goals. If I were in their shoes, I would also want to highlight that the clinicians, in their haste to accept the Love's story uncritically, had arrived at faulty conclusions via a clinical version of "garbage in, garbage out."

My reaction to this emerging focus on credibility serves as a study in ambivalence. Part of me had no stomach for building a case that Jonathan and his mother may have committed sins of omission, if not commission. Even if some of the information I had reviewed might not have been wholly accurate, it nonetheless still described the life of a non-disabled individual. Why expend the time and effort to undermine the plaintiff's credibility if we already had sufficient grounds for arguing the case based on the available evidence? The answer the LSAC lawyers gave was identical to what I have heard from many others in similar circumstances: "Because you never know what a judge will do, you hit them with absolutely everything you have at your disposal." My sense is that lawyers are trained to assume that judges will not always react as anticipated.

Endeavoring to discredit the witness also felt like far less noble a strategy than the one the case followed initially. Like it or not, many people are apt to shave the truth if it gives them an advantage. I imagine that most parents will do just about anything to make life better for their children, even if that involves some fact stretching along the way. Sticking to legal arguments, especially given their strength in this case, struck me as a far cleaner method.

Opposing those more noble sentiments were others rooted in the sense that the court should know the downsides of letting an individual "self-qualify" as impaired under the Americans with Disabilities Act. The gulf between Mr. Love's account and what emerged from contemporaneous records validated the message some of us had been preaching for years: Beware of self-report as the sole basis for formulating a diagnosis of ADHD. By carefully documenting the inaccuracies of the plaintiff's story, the LSAC attorneys provided the quintessential object lesson in a "trust but verify" strategy for clinical assessment. Indeed, my PowerPoint presentation on the diagnosis of ADHD soon included slides that contrasted what the Loves told clinicians with the reality as portrayed by external evidence. The discovery phase of *Love v. LSAC* offered a rare glimpse into the actual story behind an application for accommodations.

My motivations for helping to establish the facts of Love's life also sprang from ongoing research interests. For years I had been working with my colleagues, especially Drs. Larry Lewandowski and Kevin Murphy, to explore the validity of self-report in the context of ADHD evaluations for ADA accommodations. Our intent was to infuse the debate about how much to rely upon a patient's report with as much scientific data as possible. Arguments based on data are, of course, far stronger than those founded upon anecdote or personal preference. But the tale of Jonathan Love's efforts to put his worst foot forward in clinical interviews breathed life into the soberly-stated conclusions we wrote for scientific journals. He served as the poster child for research that documented the value of a comprehensive assessment.

For the record, I have been interested in the validity of self-report since I was a graduate student. The head of my program at The Ohio State University, Dr. Charles Wenar, had written an article in 1968 about the extent to which one could rely on a mother's report of details regarding pregnancy, birth, and early development. He concluded that a "good deal of past research has leaned heavily on the slenderest of reeds." What mothers reported was often inconsistent with hard data in medical records or from other independent verification. He went so far as to write, "It may well be that mothers' histories mislead more often than they illuminate."

Dr. Wenar's summary left an impression on me. If mothers were often inaccurate when reporting information as straightforward as birth weight, how exclusively should we rely on their reports about socioemotional development, academic potential/progress, and interpersonal functioning? Data on the breach between self-report and reality justified casting a wide net when fishing for clinical information.

Research over the next four decades has only served to confirm the general unreliability of self-report. While the evidence for this stance is widespread, some of the best examples come from child psychiatric research. For instance, it has been firmly established that even when self-report is formatted in a behavior rating scale, it can prove inaccurate. An especially well-documented influence on those ratings is maternal depression. Simply put, depressed mothers are apt to over-rate the breadth and severity of their children's problem behavior, a predictable finding given the clouding impact of depression's hallmark irritability, pessimism, and sadness. Fathers with substance abuse problems are also prone to gin up the severity of a child's problems. Generally speaking, parents with troubles of their own will tend to overreact to what may be typical childhood behavior.

As for reports by the patients themselves, the literature also discourages an over-abundance of confidence in their reliability. For example, the complaints about cognitive problems that people entering substance abuse programs report are often tied more to their level of depression than to their actual performance on laboratory measures of cognitive functioning. In other words, they report being more impaired than their test results would indicate. Researchers have found the same disconnect between self-report and objective assessment in groups of individuals with bipolar disorder, schizophrenia, cocaine addition, brain injury, bulimia, and personality disorders. To varying degrees, patients will over- or under-report their symptoms.

To be fair, patients with psychiatric or medical problems are not the only ones whose accounts can be inaccurate. Studies indicate that students are prone to err when they list grade point averages and SAT scores on applications. In one 2007 study by Dr. Richard Mayer and colleagues, students tended to over-report their SAT scores by an average of twenty-five points. Not surprisingly, those students with the lowest actual SAT scores were most likely to inflate their scores on applications.

The scientific literature on self-report in the ADHD realm is intriguing and somewhat complex. Individuals who have been diagnosed with ADHD by research criteria are likely to under-report their symptoms compared to how others rate them. Extremely impulsive people are less apt to reflect on the consequences of their actions. They often fail to consider how their behavior might have caused problems for themselves or others. In psychological parlance, they demonstrate a "positive illusory bias" about their functioning when they were children and in their current circumstance. Because it is not easy for them to consider that their behavior might be problematic, adults with ADHD should be encouraged to have family members and friends participate in initial assessments and ongoing treatment evaluations.

What about the validity of accounts that adult patients give clinicians during initial evaluations? Are they accurate? Yes and no. More often than not, the patient's self-report will fall in the same general ballpark as information from other sources. However, while opinions will often converge, the level of agreement is not so high that self-ratings alone can reliably point to a diagnosis. To quote authors of an article that generally endorsed the utility of self-reports: "Reliable and valid self-report questionnaires may be especially important in data collection for research purposes, but it should be noted that in clinical work, where decisions need to be made about individual cases, nothing can supplant thorough clinical interviews and information collected from several sources" (Magnússon, P., Smári, J., Sigurðardóttir, D., Baldursson, G., Sigmundsson, J., Kristjánsson, K., Sigurðardóttir, S., Hreiðarsson, S., Sigurbjörnsdóttir, S., & Guðmundsson, O. [2006]. Validity of self-report and informant rating scales of adult adhd symptoms in comparison with a semistructured diagnostic interview. *Journal of Attention Disorders*, 9 (3), p. 502.). You will find that same conclusion restated throughout the scientific literature.

Other evidence raises warning signs about an overreliance on patient reports when conducting an ADHD evaluation. Some of the most compelling data happens to come from our own research program. In one study, we reanalyzed the data from a nonclinical sample of adults who helped to standardize an ADHD rating scale. We asked this question: To what extent do individuals in the general population report symptoms associated with this disorder? The answer? It was common for typical adults to report ADHD symptoms. Fully 25 percent endorsed at least six DSM-IV symptoms as occurring often during childhood. Twelve percent indicated that they exhibited this clinical level of ADHD symptoms currently. That number is more than double the commonly-cited prevalence rate for the disorder.

The degree to which non-ADHD adults report the incidence of specific symptoms was striking. When asked about their childhood, a third of the sample said they often fidgeted with their hands or feet, lost things for tasks or activities, had difficulty organizing themselves for tasks, and felt on the go "as if driven by a motor." About a quarter of the group said they failed to give close attention to details, had difficulty sustaining attention, blurted out answers, and did not listen when spoken to directly.

Those percentages were also higher than predicted when the study participants were asked about their functioning during adulthood. The estimate for one symptom was especially high: Forty percent of these typical adults indicated that they often felt on the go "as if driven by a motor." Roughly a quarter reported often feeling restless and fidgety. Because it is not uncommon for people to report that they frequently experience ADHD symptoms in their lives, clinicians would do well to corroborate that those symptoms are associated with actual impairment.

We reached similar conclusions after collecting rating scale data on 534 typical college students (Lewandowski, et al., 2008). About 4 percent of the sample endorsed clinical levels of ADHD symptoms. Five percent indicated equally significant levels of LD symptoms.

Endorsements of particular symptoms amongst these college students were compelling. Judge for yourself:

Rarely read in my spare time	59%
Easily distracted	54%
Read material over and over	53%
Work harder than most people to get good grades	44%
Do not perform well on timed tests	45%

According to these data, it is normal for college students to complain about being distracted, having to work hard, and struggling on timed tests and while reading. Unless we want to diagnose half the college student population as having a psychiatric disorder, we should be hesitant to rely entirely on their personal accounts for diagnostic direction.

My point here is not that all information gathered through self-report should be dismissed as so much hooey or that mothers are weapons of mass distortion. What a person reports is of obvious significance in the diagnostic process, even for those patients who are most prone to be inaccurate in their accounts. It is more that self-report alone is a shaky foundation for a diagnostic determination. As we will see, that foundation is at its shakiest when the reporter has a desired outcome in mind.

Now to the question that must have confronted the LSAC defense team: How far off was the information that Mr. Love and his mother presented to the clinicians he hired to help him gain accommodations? Did he hide important information, exaggerate elements of his history, and otherwise tailor his account in an effort to present himself as disabled? And how many of the inaccuracies that surfaced during the course of the litigation were honest mistakes, minor distortions, or the consequence of a concerted effort to misrepresent the facts?

Some of the Love-generated inaccuracies were more clearly innocent than others. One concerned Mrs. Love's report to both Drs. Brunn and Van Auken that her son's abilities were "especially low in reading comprehension" during elementary and middle school. This characterization served as a basis for clinicians asserting the Jonathan Love had a longstanding history of learning problems. It also found its way into the declaration that Dr. Runyan submitted as part of the litigation.

The actual test profiles, obtained by the LSAC during the discovery phase of the lawsuit, show that Mrs. Love's account was mistaken. According to national norms, his scores on the reading comprehension section of the Iowa Tests of Basic Skills were in the average- to the high-average range for every year from third through eighth grade. He never had a below-average score on a standardized reading test administered while he was in elementary or middle school.

How did Mrs. Love arrive at the conclusion that his reading comprehension scores were low? The interchange between her and Ms. Leopold-Leventhal at the deposition offers an explanation:

Q. Well, sitting here today, which of those scores are below average?
A. Well, Vocabulary and Reading. Anything that's close to the 50th percentile because ... to me a 50 is failing.
Q. Okay. So that's what you base that on?
A. Correct ...

Q. What else would have been below average to you?
A. Well, Reading, here you are at 50.
Q. That's below average, right?
A. Correct. 50 on Vocabulary. I consider that below average . . .
Q. All of those scores are in the below 60 percentile, correct?
A. Correct.
Q. And that's why you concluded that they were below average, correct?
A. Correct.

Judging from her testimony, Mrs. Love made an honest mistake. She confused grade scores (where a 50 would be failing) with percentiles (where a 50 is average). Had the clinicians waited for those records, they perhaps would have arrived at different conclusions. Dr. Van Auken testified as much in his deposition:

Q. Do you believe that having that information from, let's say, elementary and middle school, as far as how Mr. Love scored on standardized reading tests when he was in sixth, seventh, and eighth grade, might have provided you with a more complete picture of his reading comprehension ability?
A. Given time to complete a comprehensive evaluation, and the more data that you have the better.
Q. So, your answer is yes?
A. Yes.

Certain questions leap to mind (at least to mine) when pondering the approach these clinicians took to data gathering. How could Dr. Van Auken verify Jonathan Love's purported disability based upon anything less than a full evaluation? What pushed Dr. Brunn to submit her report before she got all the records required? Is it legitimate to sign a quasi-legal document supporting accommodations without having collected sufficient data? Would an orthopedist assert that a patient qualified for workman's compensation before making sure he looked at all the medical information?

The lack of diligence cannot be fairly justified by circumstance. Mrs. Love actually had the score reports and other academic records in a box at home. She claimed she forgot she had them and that Dr. Brunn failed to ask her specifically for these kinds of records. Also, despite Mrs. Love's report that it would take too long to get the school records from storage, the LSAC attorneys received them in less than a week after submitting a request.

Perhaps part of the reason stems from Jonathan Love's insistence on getting the results quickly. Both clinicians seemed intent on acceding to his wishes. When asked in the deposition why she never received records, Dr. Brunn responded as follows:

Q. And was she able to obtain those records for you?
A. No. She said that they were archived. We were – or Jonathan was in a hurry to have the report done and I decided that … he probably had had difficulty in the past, and I didn't worry about it too much. I went ahead and wrote the report …
Q. And do you believe that your evaluation of Jonathan was compromised in any way by not having his elementary school records?
A. No.
Q. And why's that?
A. Well, because I believed, and still believe, that Ms. Love was reliable in her report, and I don't have that information when I'm evaluating adults very often, unfortunately. It would be nice to have, but I don't routinely have it. And so I'm accustomed to accepting reports of people who appear to be reliable.

According to Dr. Van Auken, Jonathan Love sought his services only so that he could administer a reading test while the patient was medicated. The clinician did insist on a clinical interview and that Mrs. Love complete some questionnaires. But, for the most part, he accepted the two prior evaluations, as he testified:

He had already completed a comprehensive evaluation looking at learning disabilities issues. And, so, given that he had been tested within the recent past, and he specifically indicated that, due to cost issues and issues of wanting to expedite the examination, that he didn't want to have a redo on those tests, I simply took the report that he had from the past and looked at that – the two reports, actually, that he had.

In addition to inaccuracies tied to confusion about statistics were many more born of exaggeration. For example, Mrs. Love reported to Dr. Brunn that every one of Jonathan's teachers had to move his chair to the front row. She repeated that claim in her legal declaration when she wrote, "In elementary school, Jonathan's teachers informed me that they had to change Jonathan's seating placement in class to help him focus, which became a technique used by all of Jonathan's teachers throughout his elementary and secondary education." Ms. Leopold-Leventhal asked her about that statement in the deposition:

Q. You have a statement in here that all of Jonathan's teachers throughout elementary and secondary education changed his seat. Is that accurate? Every single teacher changed his seat?

A. Almost every single teacher, yes, had him sit in the front of the class where he would be less distracted, yes.

Q. In the front of the class?

A. Right, where he was less distracted or away from the window.

Q. And that was true throughout high school?

A. Yes, a number of them.

Q. Well, a number or all of them?

A. I mean, I'm not going to say every single one of them.

Q. Well, that's what you say here and that's what I'm trying to find out. That seems a bit of an exaggeration, that every single teacher in high school changed his seat. But if that's true, that's okay, because I'll call them. But I don't think that's true . . .

A. I'm sure there were some that didn't.

Q. I'm just asking you a couple of months after your declaration to name some of them in high school who changed his seat because you said every single one did. Can you think of one? Can you think of any?

A. I can't remember their names. I'm sorry.

True to her word, Mrs. Leopold-Leventhal deposed a number of the plaintiff's teachers. At trial, she reviewed that testimony with Mrs. Love:

Q. And are you aware that Ms. Colbert testified that your son sat in the back of the room, and she never changed his seat to help him focus?

A. Yes.

Q. And are you aware that Ms. Yates, your son's twelfth grade English teacher, testified that she never had to move his seat in order to help him focus?

A. Yes.

Q. And are you aware that Mr. Anderson testified that he never asked for the seat to be changed, and he had that opportunity several times in the semester?

A. I didn't know that he said that, but –

Q. Okay. So you would agree with me at least that all of Jonathan's teachers throughout secondary and elementary education didn't change his seat, just some of them. Correct?

A. Yes. That was a mistake.

Another assertion that found its way into the lore of Jonathan Love's educational history is that he required constant tutoring. In his report, Dr. Van Auken wrote that Mr. Love received tutorial assistance for "seventy or eighty percent" of his classes. Dr. Runyan mentioned in her declaration and testimony that he had "extensive tutoring." However, at his deposition, Mr. Love was unable to identify the names of any of his tutors. His mother was similarly unable to remember details regarding his tutoring other than vaguely recalling that he needed it primarily in reading and math. The plaintiffs could not produce any evidence that he was provided more tutoring than other students at his prep school. While he may have been tutored, no evidence existed that it was, as Ms. Joanne Simon characterized it at my deposition, "consistent tutoring every year, every week, throughout elementary and high school."

Another key element of the history Mr. Love and his mother gave clinicians was that teachers and professors routinely offered him extra time on exams throughout his educational career. That assertion became yet another part of the clinical mantra the clinicians used in their justification for why he should received accommodations on the LSAT. This is what Mr. Love wrote in his declaration:

> In high school I was afforded extra time to finish tests and important in-class assignments because I was unable to complete them during the standard time limits. Similarly, many of my Baylor professors voluntarily provided me with extended time on examinations in my reading intensive courses. During my junior year at Baylor, I learned about the formal accommodation process offered by Baylor's Office for Access and Learning Accommodations. At that point, however, I did not think it was necessary to register for formal accommodations because my professors were willing to provide accommodations informally.

He told Dr. Van Auken that a number of professors at Baylor provided an informal accommodation of "extended time on tests of as much time as I needed or would allow testing to be completed in faculty offices." For example, he claimed in writing on LSAC forms that a Professor Delaney gave him extra time on exams in two courses at Baylor University. However, in a deposition, Professor Delaney indicated that he routinely advised the entire class on the first day that he could not give extra time on tests to students unless they went through the Baylor Accommodations Office and were formally identified as in need of special accommodations. He was adamant that Mr. Love was never allowed extra time. Under intense cross examination at trial, Mr. Love indicated that he "might have been mistaken" about having received extra time to take those examinations.

Parenthetically, Dr. Brunn saw these "mistakes" as further proof that Jonathan Love had ADHD. According to her, those mischaracterizations were because of his ADHD-related problem "getting the details right when he's asked spur of the moment to recall. He may mix things up." Apparently he was so impaired that he could not be relied upon to provide accurate information, even on a legal declaration.

More important than the percentage of courses Mr. Love took for which he was allowed extra time stands the reality that he never had that accommodation on any examination in his academic career until his took the GMAT in 2005. Those exams included all standardized tests in middle school and high school, the SAT, ACT, and LSAT, as well as all of his courses at Baylor and Notre Dame. Prior to his LSAT and GMAT applications, he never sought formal accommodations on any examination despite knowing he had that option. For example, he did not apply for accommodations on the Texas and Louisiana real estate examinations even though the application materials clearly stated that the test centers were equipped to provide access and reasonable accommodations under the Americans with Disabilities Act. He passed both timed examinations on the first attempt, a success he did not report to Dr. Brunn.

What also emerged from depositions provided by three of his former high school teachers was how ably Jonathan Love handled a challenging academic program. They all saw him as a solid, respectful student. When Ms. Leopold-Leventhal asked them whether Mr. Love showed symptoms associated with ADHD, they all responded in the negative. His twelfth-grade English teacher, Ms. Margaret Yates, provided the court with a general sense of the English curriculum for that year. It included *Beowulf*, *Gilgamesh*, *The Iliad of Homer*, *Canterbury Tales*, Border Ballads, *Hamlet*, and *Macbeth* along with works by Swift, Pope, Defoe, Wordsworth, Byron, Shelley, Keats, Tennyson, Browning, Donne, Jonson, Marvell, Herrick, and Milton. The summer reading list included *A Picture of Dorian Gray* and *A Tale of Two Cities*. According to Ms. Yates, Mr. Love handled this daunting survey of English literature without the need for accommodations:

Q. As far as you can recall, did Mr. Love always complete the assignments in your class on time?

A. Yes.

Q. And as far as you can recall, Mr. Love or his mother never asked you for additional time to allow Jonathan to complete assignments. Is that a fair statement?

A. That's a fair statement ...

Q. Did Mr. Love or his mother ever ask you to change Jonathan's seat to help him focus in class?

A. I don't recall that.

Q. Did you ever speak with Mr. Love's guidance counselor while Mr. Love was a student at Loyola Prep about his having difficulty on reading assignments or focusing in class?

A. I don't recall doing that.

Now we arrive at what became a central focus of the effort to establish the truth about Jonathan Love's purported treatment for ADHD. In his interviews with Drs. Brunn and Van Auken, Mr. Love indicated that he routinely took stimulant medication to manage his ADHD symptoms. As he described it during his deposition, "I needed to take the Adderall to make myself sit down and study. And that was the majority of the times I would take it for different testing environments." Dr. Van Auken provided further details in his original report:

> Currently, Jonathan notes that he "mainly takes the regular Adderall" (10 mg, q.d.) in the mornings and on "long days, at testing times," he will take Adderall XR (30 mg). These medications are perceived as very helpful. Jonathan reported that he has "tried other" medications including Concerta, but found Adderall to be more effective.

That an individual requires medication to study and take examinations is regarded by most as suggestive of a legitimate disability. After all, it would be hard to understand why someone would take heart medication if he did not have a heart problem or wear a cast if his arm were not broken. If Jonathan Love routinely took this medication and derived significant benefit from treatment, would that not support his claim that he has an abnormality that requires accommodations?

Over the Thanksgiving weekend, I watched the video of Mr. Love's deposition from the prior week in which he described how he came to take Adderall. The testimony went as follows:

Q. And Dr. Davenport was the first doctor to diagnose you with ADHD. Is that correct?
A. I believe he was the first, yes.
Q. And did he prescribe Adderall for you?
A. I believe he did.
Q. In what dosage?
A. I can't remember . . .
Q. You never returned to Dr. Davenport after that initial visit, isn't that right?
A. Correct.
Q. Who continued to prescribe the Adderall for you after your – Dr. Davenport prescribed it the first time?
A. I'm unaware. My mother generally took care of all of that information for me.
Q. What does that mean?
A. My mother just simply would obtain the Adderall from the doctors I would go to, prescribed it for me.

When I heard that portion of the deposition, I knew right away that Dr. Davenport could not have prescribed the medication. As a Louisiana-based psychologist in 2000, he would not have had legal authority to prescribe (the state did pass a law allowing psychologists with specialized training to prescribe certain medication, but that change did not take effect until 2004). If Mr. Love were prescribed medications, Dr. Davenport's signature was not on the prescription pad.

Another element of the testimony struck me as improbable. Because it is a stimulant medication, Adderall is classified as a schedule II narcotic under the Controlled Substances Act of 1970. Medications with that designation fall under strict rules for prescribing, including a prohibition against writing prescriptions with a refill option. Also, until December 2007, prescribers could only write scripts for a thirty-day supply of medication. Therefore, to have taken Adderall routinely, Mr. Love would have had to attend monthly appointments with a physician or nurse in the office. However, he did not remember the names of any doctors he went to for the purpose of acquiring more Adderall. According to him, his mother generally arranged to have the prescriptions filled. But his mother similarly could not recall any of the providers she supposedly consulted to secure stimulant medication for her son.

How likely is it that a physician would write years-worth of prescriptions for stimulant medications without ever seeing the patient? Not very. Most would regard that practice as falling far outside an accepted standard of care. In fact, every psychiatrist and pediatrician I have asked said that prescribing in such manner would be considered unethical. A mother simply cannot call up for refills of a schedule II narcotic with known side effects the way she might request a prescription for a nasal decongestant. Besides, at trial, she testified that she picked up prescriptions "Maybe every six months or a year, I don't know." Her son could not have had many pills at his disposal.

Without thinking much of it, I wrote Ms. Leopold-Leventhal about my suspicions: If Mr. Love took Adderall at all, it probably was not on a regular basis because he could not have amassed the necessary number of pills without visiting a prescriber about every month. Drs. Brunn and Van Auken appeared to be operating under the impression he took the medication regularly when, in reality, he must have taken it on relatively rare occasions (he eventually acknowledged that he used it "very sporadically"). The explanation that his mother was routinely able to arrange for the prescriptions to be filled was also improbable. And, regardless, it was not Dr. Davenport who wrote those first prescriptions; he simply was not in a position to do so. The entire story seemed curious.

While my reaction to the testimony about medication was mild, Ms. Leopold-Leventhal's was anything but muted. The information I had relayed appeared to firmly substantiate her suspicion that the Loves had grossly overstated how much he took medication to treat his ADHD symptoms. While she was not familiar with the nuances involved in prescribing stimulants, it struck her as odd that Love could not remember seeing anyone around the management of his medication. I imagine that her litigator's spirit soared at the prospect of dismantling his story at trial.

The subpoenas she issued for medical records and the like provided her with all the makings of a wrecking ball she could take to Love's account. She was able to prove that none of the physicians he identified as providing him medical care prescribed him stimulant medications. The evidence also showed that when providers asked on medical information forms whether he was taking any medications, Mr. Love responded that he was not. None of the medical doctors he saw for physical complaints between the years 2000 and 2006 were aware he was prescribed Adderall. In fact, the only script the plaintiffs could provide prior to the trial was written three days after Jonathan Love's deposition in 2006.

It was not just medical treatment that Mr. Love shied away from over the year. He never sought any other form of treatment. At no point did he ever consult a therapist, life skills coach, or other professional to help him cope with his purported disorder. The only reason he went to a mental health professional was to secure accommodations on testing.

Yet another overstatement emerged in Mr. Love's LSAT application for accommodations and the accompanying psychologists' reports. A family history of ADHD, while not diagnostic of the disorder, is considered to be suggestive. According to research, ADHD is highly heritable, roughly at the same level as hair color and height. Jonathan Love indicated to the providers that he had an uncle and sister who had been diagnosed with ADHD. His statement led to Dr. Brunn writing that he had a "strong family history of ADHD." His mother extended the list of family members who were diagnosed or who showed signs of the disorder. These included her ex-husband, sister, three of Jonathan's cousins, and, yes, Mrs. Love herself. However, with the possible exception of Jonathan's sister, none of these family members were formally diagnosed as having ADHD. Even the sister's status was unclear given that she was not identified until college (by the same psychologist who initially diagnosed Jonathan as having ADHD). The clinicians assumed a strong family history when, in reality, the evidence for that conclusion was weak.

And now to the domain that most occupied my attentions during preparation for the trial. The reader will remember that an early childhood history of ADHD behavior is required for the diagnosis of the disorder. Someone simply does not "come down" with ADHD after puberty. Like Chicago voters of yore, the symptoms show up early and often. In Jonathan's case, the clinicians felt that this early-onset criterion was satisfied when Mrs. Love wrote to Dr. Brunn that her son was "extremely ADD" as a child. On a form she completed for Dr. Van Auken, she elaborated as follows:

> Jonathan has always shown the signs of ADHD. Even though his symptoms were present since childhood, Jonathan was not tested until high school because he always received extended time on homework assignments, tests, etc. without having to show a record of his impairment.

In her deposition and at trial, she painted a picture of an abnormally scatterbrained and disorganized child who required an inordinate amount of supervision and attention:

> Because Jonathan was so easily distracted, it was difficult to keep him on track both at home and with his school work ... Jonathan was never a discipline problem in school, but was generally forgetful, easily distracted in class, and was regularly caught daydreaming by his teachers ... Jonathan is, I'm sure every one knows, he gets very distracted, he is very forgetful. Jonathan is very dazed at times, he is very slow with recalling where he has left something, you know, he will leave things laying around, he will forget things, he is very – he gets extremely distracted, that has been a huge problem for Jonathan ever since he has been a young child.

These sorts of characterizations were all that Drs. Brunn and Van Auken required for them to verify an early-onset of symptoms.

How accurate was Mrs. Love's portrayal of her son's childhood? Is there any evidence that he was abnormally inattentive or impulsive? Did he meet the DSM-IV's criterion that the patient show impairment due to ADHD symptoms from an early age?

Even Mrs. Love's own responses on Dr. Van Auken's questionnaires are inconsistent with her depiction of him as unusually distractible and overactive. In the "Behavior/Temperament" section of the Behavior Assessment System for Children, Second Edition, Structured Developmental History form, she marked "No" to items that asked if her child, when younger, had a short attention span, lacked self-control, seemed impulsive, or had trouble calming down. She indicated that he had no problems with reading or math, getting along with others, or maintaining his mood.

The statement that literally made my jaw drop came in response to the item, "What do you find most difficult about raising this child?" Her answer was stunning: "Nothing. He was a blessing and a very good child. Very respectful as well." If you were to ask that question to a parent of a child with ADHD, you would first want to make sure you offered extra sheets of paper; the two lines allocated for that item would only suffice if the parent were to write something succinct, like "Everything." You might also want to offer an extra pen in case the one you provided ran out of ink or Kleenex to dry the tears. When you read the response, I guarantee that you would never see the words "very good child" other than perhaps in the sentence, "Although his sister is a very good child, he won't listen or follow directions."

As for the parent describing the child as a "blessing," let me report what a good-humored mother told me at an ADHD parent support group when I asked if, on a behavior rating form, she would use that descriptor to characterize her son. "Sure," she said. "But only when he's sleeping. The rest of the time he's more like the spawn of the devil."

While Mrs. Love saw no inconsistency between claims that her son had a longstanding history of ADHD symptoms and the description of him as a "blessing and a very good child," the defense attorneys were less accepting. At both the deposition and trial, they kept asking how she could mark on the forms that he had no problems reading or attending but still assert he could not read or attend. She ultimately fell back on two lines of defense. She first claimed that, while he was extremely ADHD, he showed "determination, perseverance, hard work and a solid work ethic. He would stick with it until he got it done." She also said, "He is very driven. He is the type of child that when he puts his mind on something, he pretty much isn't going to stop until he gets there, no matter how hard it is for him to do that."

What Mrs. Love is admitting, of course, is that her son shows strength in exactly the area someone with ADHD would demonstrate the greatest weakness, that is, task persistence. At the core of ADHD is the inability to manage routine tasks that require diligence in the face of distraction. If you can overcome whatever distractibility you might experience through persistence and without unusual levels of outside supervision, you do not have ADHD. You might have a bad case of being human, but you do not have ADHD.

Mrs. Love's other explanation for her incompatible description of Jonathan's childhood was that, because of her own ADHD, she rushed through the forms without careful consideration. Here is how she explained it at her deposition:

Q. Okay. So you put incorrect information on this form that you were filling out for Dr. Van Auken?
A. It wasn't intentional.

Q. Well, what was the cause of it?

A. I could have very easily been distracted ... because if I hadn't been dis-tracted I would have never put [that he didn't have] a short attention span.

Q. Didn't you take this seriously?

A. Yes, I did. But, I mean, sometimes things just get – you know, I guess my own attention deficit comes out.

If you were to see how Mrs. Love completed the forms, you would not arrive at the conclusion that she was hasty. Her penmanship is excellent and even the circles she drew around responses were carefully drawn.

Leaving aside Mrs. Love's narrative, what in the school records would support the notion that he was impaired because of ADHD symptoms? The answer is simple. Absolutely nothing in the report cards suggests even a hint of abnormal functioning associated with ADHD or any other problem. His "conduct" marks in the early grades were uniformly positive. For example, in the sixteen grading periods between first and fourth grades, he received all but one "Good" for the item, "Completes work in a reasonable time." That single instance of a lower score was a "Satisfactory." He received simi-lar kudos for the item "Understands and Follows Directions." His marks for "Listens Attentively" were only slightly lower in that he received a "Needs Improvement" score at the beginning of two years. By the second grading period, he was in the satisfactory range across the board.

As for his grades, here again his report cards reflect solid achievement. For the first four years of elementary school, he never earned lower than a "B." His grades in reading would make a mother and father proud in that they were always "A" or "B." He never earned lower than an "A" in spell-ing. Out of 144 grades during elementary school, he had 102 As, 40 Bs, and 2 Cs. Nothing whatsoever in the record points to a child so impulsive, inat-tentive, and disorganized that he was unable to acquire academic skills and manage classroom demands. The Love's contention that he was "Extremely ADD" and a poor reader fail to pass muster in the light of the contempora-neous record.

During the course of trial preparation(s), the defense attorneys had the idea to subpoena Mr. Love's applications to graduate school. They must have been curious how he presented himself when the goal was to convey competence rather than limitation. His self-descriptions could not have been more disparate. When he wanted to portray himself as disabled, he was a hapless soul beset with disabilities that stood between him and a nor-mal life. When he intended to present himself as perfectly suited for admis-sion to a top business school, he was competence personified. It caught my eye when, in an essay, he highlighted his "flexibility to change and ability to manage and multitask." After indicating that he would be graduating with a double major in Finance and Real Estate, he touted his drive for success and the benefits of his business experience at Nader's Gallery, an art frame and furniture store in Shreveport:

> After entering the company in 2003 as developer and manager of the furniture side of the business, sales doubled. I attribute this jump in sales to two things, market share and e-commerce. I introduced one of the only modern furniture lines in Shreveport capturing the majority of the market. As sales soared I introduced the merchandise online, which has proven to be successful. I realize that the retail market I have become accustomed to is much different than the financial market, but I see many similarities including customer and client relations, the need for multitasking and an entrepreneurial attitude, and raw motivation . . . Ultimately, as a manager of employees and sales as well as and an initiator of a new business, I realize how important flexibility is. In today's changing, global world, it is now more important than ever to be flexible and market driven. My ability to multitask and partition responsibilities among employees is crucial in the business environment, and should prove beneficial ultimately in my financial career.

Accompanying his application were recommendation forms completed by the owners of Nader's Gallery. On his application, Mr. Love indicated that he worked at this firm for fifty plus hours per week over thirty-two months at an ending salary of $40,000 per year. Each recommender gave him "superior" or "excellent" ratings on all checklist items including: managerial promise, leadership, maturity, confidence, ability to meet deadlines, ability to work with others, and intellectual ability. The comments that accompanied those ratings were glowing:

> Mr. Love has been our best manager of production and sales. He introduced our furniture line which doubled our sales. He also initiated, created, and maintains our website and e-commerce. Most importantly, his managerial skills are superb. He is able to multitask and stay productive through the day.

The other owner shared similar sentiments:

> Jonathan's ability to manage employees and lead the organization is superior. He has not only been an excellent manager, but he has also introduced new ideas to the company and helped drastically increase sales in the past few years. Jonathan's employees work extremely well under his supervision.

To say the least, these are not descriptions of an individual plagued by an inability to plan, organize, and stay focused. We have here a picture of

Jonathan Love the Superstar: multitasking, ambitious, and supremely competent.

Or do we? The recommendations were submitted by co-owners Edward Nader and Margaret Nader. The latter indicated that she knew the applicant as her employee for more than two years. To be exact, she knew him at that point for 24 years because Margaret Nader is Jonathan Love's mother. Although she used her married name, "Margaret Love," on her business card, driver's license, tax returns, business filings, and legal declarations, she signed her maiden name to submit the recommendation to Notre Dame. And, of course, Edward Nader is Jonathan's uncle, a family tie he too failed to disclose on the recommendation form, even though it provided a box labeled "Other" to characterize the nature of the relationship.

The application also contained inaccuracies. It was established during the litigation that: 1) his work at the gallery was part-time and episodic; 2) he had no formal responsibilities for staff supervision or management; 3) he played no role in business planning or expansion; 4) he mostly worked on the Web site; and 5) Jonathan was never paid a salary. His contribution to the introduction of the new furniture line was to post images of the products on the Internet.

Mrs. Love and her brother submitted recommendations to other graduate schools, including the New York University (NYU) Stern School of Business, again without disclosing their family ties. Mrs. Love, writing as Margaret Nader, wrote that "Jonathan helped save this business in 2002 when he implemented the website for the company, which stimulated sales drastically. He was promoted to store manager and has performed beyond our expectations ever since." It never happened. The record shows that he was hardly even around the store during that period.

In the deposition and at trial, Mrs. Love portrayed Jonathan's functioning in her company differently than she did writing as Margaret Nader. Her description of Jonathan's work ethic was especially inconsistent with her ratings of him in the excellent to superior range. For example, she was asked about his ability to multitask on the job:

Q. And do you agree with [Edward Nader's statement on the Notre Dame form] that Jonathan was able to multitask while at Nader's Gallery and continued to stay productive during the day?
A. Not really.
Q. Why not?
A. He gets very distracted and he would start something, lay it down, start something, lay it down. And I guess that was a lot. He would just – he would start a project and get distracted, but then he would finally go

back and complete it after a long period of time or working at it or sticking with it. But I guess I wouldn't, as far as multitasking, I didn't perceive it like that.

Mrs. Love's testimony during the trial made it even harder to judge the reality of Jonathan's job performance. On the NYU application, she wrote in response to a question that asked about areas in which the applicant could improve, "Jonathan is able to manage all of his responsibilities with ease. There really isn't an area that I can think of that Jonathan could greatly improve." Contrast that statement with her response to a question from the plaintiff's attorney during direct examination:

Q. When Jonathan worked at Nader's Gallery, were there any times when his ADHD interfered with the performance of his job responsibilities?
A. He was very haphazard there also. I mean, Jonathan would have a terrible habit of laying things around. He would start to fax something, forget that he was faxing and then walk off and then have to come back later and find it ... if the phone would ring or someone would come in, a customer could see in there, they would ask him a question, he would get off track, leave things laying around. He would start to, you know, help us to hang things on the wall, or move furniture and he would leave it half done ...

Within a few minutes of that statement, she lauded his contributions to the business: "I personally believe he did an excellent job. He increased our sales and he got us a tremendous amount of exposure, which ultimately was very helpful for the bottom line." It is therefore anyone's guess how well Jonathan functioned on the job. But that is the point. Relying on the report of parties who have a conflict of interest is a surefire way to draw the wrong conclusions.

The final issue of credibility that emerges from this case concerns discrepant results on psychological testing. Analyzing those discrepancies requires asking questions that Jonathan Love's clinicians did not entertain: Did the plaintiff's uneven performance in various testing circumstances perhaps reflect an effort to feign impairment? And how do clinicians generally determine if a patient is malingering?

Before delving into research on malingering, let me first describe how the topic emerged. Mr. Love took the Nelson-Denny Reading Test three times. His first encounter was when Dr. Brunn administered it to him during the 2004 evaluation. He was unmedicated at the time. When he visited Dr. Van Auken in 2006, it was with the express intent of having him administer the test to him when he was on medication. Dr. Van Auken administered the test under both standard and extended time conditions.

Mr. Love's performance for all three administrations was extremely poor. Medication or not, in Texas or Indiana, with or without extended time, his scores were mostly in the first percentile compared to college students. His score on the reading comprehension section of the test fell roughly at the fourth-grade level. None of the scores exceeded what would be expected of an eighth grader. According to results of the Nelson-Denny, this graduate of Baylor University with a double major in Finance and Real Estate, this student in good standing in the MBA program at Notre Dame University, this future enrollee in law school was unable to read better than most children in middle school.

The Nelson-Denny scores were at odds not only with his scholastic achievement but with other diagnostic tests. For example, when Mr. Love was first evaluated in 2000 by a Micheal Davenport, Ph.D., he was administered Passage Comprehension of the Woodcock Johnson Achievement Battery – Revised Form. His performance was in the average range. So too was his score on the Brunn-administered "Broad Reading" index of the Woodcock-Johnson, not to mention every single standardized reading test he took from third through eighth grade as well as the verbal portion of the SAT college entrance examination.

The Nelson-Denny score, because it was so discrepant from results of other tests, fit the bill as an "outlier." It stood out like a psychometric sore thumb when compared to other indices. Moreover, it is impossible to imagine that someone with as limited a vocabulary and who read that slowly and with as little understanding of the material could graduate from college, let alone earn average scores on professional entrance examinations with high demand for reading. It would be as if someone almost flunked a test of running speed right before he won a 100-yard dash. The running test would not jibe with reality.

This break between test scores and reality extended to his mathematical abilities. Dr. Brunn had also diagnosed Mr. Love with an "Academic Fluency Disorder" based, in part, on his poor performance on speeded math tests. Ms. Leopold-Leventhal asked the psychologist about her diagnosis:

Q. So, after high school Mr. Love goes on to complete a four-year degree program at Baylor, and he completes courses like calculus and pre-calculus and quantitative methods, correct?
A. That's correct.
Q. Mr. Love testified he never received extended time on any of those math courses at Baylor, is that your understanding Doctor?

A. Yes.

Q. Six months after graduation with a dual degree from Baylor, Mr. Love takes a math test with you with simple addition, simple multiplication, and simple subtraction and he scores at a fourth-grade level, Dr. Brunn?

A. That is correct.

Q. Given all of this information that we've just discussed, you didn't question whether there was a motivational effort on Mr. Love's part to intentionally obtain a low score on the math fluency test, so that you would recommend more time for him on the GMAT?

A. No, I didn't.

In her report, Dr. Brunn did acknowledge the existence of a disconnect between psychological test scores and performance on timed examinations. She wrote: "Given these scores, Jonathan has done surprisingly well on standardized testing." How did she reconcile this discrepancy? Not by dismissing the Nelson-Denny scores as errant or by exploring the possibility that Mr. Love's motivation to perform well on this test might have been low. She instead claimed that he earned higher LSAT scores because he must have been able to practice. In her words, "Strong preparation for such testing undoubtedly has helped him achieve to the extent that he has without accommodations." She testified similarly at trial:

Q. Do you have an opinion as to how Jonathan could have scored average on the LSAT under standard conditions, despite his impairment?

A. I think he was very well prepared for the test. He had practiced and he knew what kinds of questions to expect, and he did the best he could.

Her argument was that the LSAT prep courses he took somehow helped him overcome profound deficits in vocabulary, reading speed, and comprehension. Her testimony also implied that someone could study the likely content of an LSAT administration. Both assertions are false. Those courses do not teach someone how to read better, nor do students learn about material that will appear on the test. They learn about the format of the exam, test-taking strategies, and the sorts of items that will appear, but they have no way of studying reading passages prior to the test. Those reading passages can cover any topic. Dr. Dempsey from the LSAC explained it to the judge in this fashion:

Q. There was also a bit of testimony from, I believe, Dr. Brunn that Mr. Love would be able to study for the LSAT and that would assist Mr. Love in obtaining the score that he received October 2003. Are you able to agree or disagree with that statement?

A. The Law School Admission Test is not based on any particular base of knowledge. A person can become familiar with the LSAT, as most test takers do prior to taking the test. But there is no way, other than to become familiar with the instructions and the types of questions that might be on it, there is no way a person could study and improve their score, because there is – there is nothing to study. It is not a factual, knowledge based assessment. It is unlike the math portion of the SAT, for example ... you can actually study for that and actually become proficient in it, but that is not true for the LSAT.

Is there any other way one could explain the stark discrepancies that surfaced in the psychological test data? Dr. Van Auken resorted to dismissing the LSAT as a "placement" test, in contrast to the (supposedly) more "diagnostic" Nelson-Denny Reading Test. But that represents a form of psychodiagnostic autism, whereby all reality rests in the isolated world of psychological test data. You simply cannot claim a test is valid when it generates conclusions out of touch with how a person functions in real life.

Dr. Golden, the other LSAC expert witness, in his court testimony, explained how he originally came to consider the Nelson-Denny data as he made his way through the packet of documentation that Mr. Love had submitted. According to his account, he first looked at the test data, which he felt "established a case for a patient who's very slow in processing information, who's reading is incredibly impaired and slow, who can't pay attention, can't focus." He continued:

I looked at the [standardized test] scores and that's where the problem started. His ACT and SAT and LSAT were all normal. And, in fact, his LSAT scores are actually stronger than his ACT and his SAT scores, which is usually the opposite. The LSAT is usually the weaker because it's the harder test. That created a situation where I had data that clearly pointed towards a major psychological disorder, but in reality, when he's tested on standardized tests [he performs well] ... We had a major contradiction that doesn't make any sense whatsoever, suggesting that the issue becomes the validity of testing ... Basically when you're a clinician and when anybody comes to you with secondary gain issues, meaning they have something to get out of the examination such as accommodations or money, you have to consider the possibility of motivational distortion. They might not try as hard or [they] do things a little slower or exaggerate. And sometimes that's not even conscious. It often can be unconscious because again they're affected by their belief that they deserve what ever they're asking for. Sometimes it is conscious.

Dr. Golden is well versed in the assessment of "motivational distortion" because of his extensive experience in forensic neuropsychology. He and his colleagues have evaluated hundreds of individuals involved in court cases around claims of neurological insult. In the world of personal injury lawsuits, worker's compensation litigation, and criminal prosecutions, clinicians are obligated to evaluate patients for the possibility that, consciously or otherwise, they are manufacturing or exaggerating their symptoms.

Researchers have provided ample justification for attending to such motivational factors. For example, in a 2002 study, Mittenburg and colleagues reported on the incidence of malingering in over thirty thousand cases evaluated by members of the American Board of Clinical Neuropsychology during a one-year period. Probable malingering and symptom exaggeration were found in 30 percent of disability evaluations, 29 percent of personal injury evaluations, 19 percent of criminal evaluations, and 8 percent of medical cases. Some have reported malingering rates as high as 40 percent in personal injury cases based on claims of brain trauma.

The idea that students would fabricate or exaggerate symptoms for the purposes of personal gain is a relatively new one in the world of learning disabilities and ADHD. Only within the past few years have relevant studies begun to emerge. Why have we clinicians arrived so late in the game? One reason may be that it took some time for students to learn that they could gain a competitive advantage by petitioning for extra time under the Americans with Disabilities Act. The law was only enacted in 1992; the right to sue because of personal injury has existed for many decades. Stimulant abuse also has been on the rise over the past decade. The field may therefore be coming to grips with the possibility that some will feign symptoms to obtain drugs.

An element of mental health culture that has kept practitioners from pursuing ADHD/LD malingering more systematically is the mistaken belief that it is easy for us to detect it through our clinical wiles. Dr. Brunn provided that rationale when she was asked about Mr. Love's motivation on psychological testing:

Q. You are aware though, Dr. Brunn, that you can administer certain tests to assess effort? In other words, the extents to which someone's score might be affected by a motivational issue or malingering?

A. Yes, I'm aware of that.

Q. Well, if you don't administer a test like that, how are you able to assess whether a person is trying as hard as he can or whether they are trying to skew responses so that they can get a desired result, a low score for example?

A. I think I would have to say that I feel I am a reasonably good judge of character, and of effort after observing all of the people I have doing tests over a period of years. I am pretty good at picking out malingerers, not perfect probably, but pretty good.

The tests Ms. Leopold-Leventhal referred to are just now beginning to find their way into ADHD and LD evaluations. They generally present the patient with tasks so easy that poor performance could only result from diminished effort. These measures are considered especially important when the person has something to gain from the identification of deficits. None of the clinicians administered such tests to Mr. Love.

The purpose of my detailed review of inaccuracies in the clinical record is not to cavil about the nuances of Mr. Love's history or credibility. The point is that the information he presented to clinicians was inaccurate in substantial ways. On each major component of an ADHD evaluation, what he and his mother gave them was inaccurate or, at best, incomplete. Unfortunately, those clinicians were also unduly willing to accept those misrepresentations at face value. If you were to read their reports and testimony, you would sense that they wanted to believe Mr. Love from the outset. Any fact inconsistent with an ADHD diagnosis was ignored or re-interpreted to their liking. A recommendation that Jonathan Love did not warrant accommodations never seemed to be in the cards; the outcome of the evaluations was clinically pre-ordained.

Is this case unique? Are Jonathan and Margaret Love more the exception than the rule? My personal opinion is that they are not alone, by any means. When incentives are high, human nature can stoop us low, whether we are actually aware of the descent or not. And the hunch that the Loves have company in how they managed the ADA request is bolstered by ample data. In addition to the studies I have already presented are many others that document how easy it is to let the facts wander. Several studies have demonstrated that it is not at all hard to feign ADHD on rating scales or on computerized tests of attention. For example, a 2004 study by Jachimowicz and Geiselman revealed a "strikingly high ability of college students to falsify a positive ADHD diagnosis by way of a self-report battery." Ninety-five percent of students shown ADHD criteria and then instructed to "fake" the symptoms on one popular rating scale, the Brown Adult ADHD Scale, would have been classified as having ADHD. With the DSM-IV's criteria in full view on the Internet, someone looking to fake a diagnosis would be well-prepared.

Combine how easy it is to malinger with a lack of accountability and the door is wide open for feigning. According to what Dr. John Ranseen from the University of Kentucky wrote in a 1998 article, less than 30 percent of the cases he reviewed for ADA accommodations included evaluations that gathered information beyond self-report. I tallied that same statistic for the last sixty-five cases I reviewed; the percentage was similar (27 percent). As long as clinicians fail to verify self-report through information from other sources, students and their parents are free to tailor their message without consequence. Until such time that clinicians alter their role from patient advocate to independent evaluator, the process will lack a mechanism for ensuring the validity of disability claims.

When I reflect upon the credibility issues that emerged in this case, I often think of a fabled interlude in medical history. In the 1820s, a young man named Alexis St. Martin was accidentally shot in the stomach. During the course of his recovery he developed a gastric fistula (an abnormal tract from the abdominal wall to the stomach). The passageway formed in such a manner that it allowed his physician, Dr. William Beaumont, to witness digestive processes that had never before been observed. Centuries of speculation were confirmed or dismissed when his doctor had the rare opportunity to see what had long been out of view.

In its own way, the case of *Love* v. *LSAC* has offered a similarly unique chance to peer at information usually obscured. To the best of my knowledge, never has an applicant's life been as painstakingly investigated as Jonathan Love's. The dogged lawyers from Eastburn & Gray spared no time or expense exploring every nook and cranny of his existence. They filled in details that Mr. Love, his mother, and the clinicians did not supply in the documentation supporting the request for accommodations. Many of those facts formed a picture of Jonathan's life that stood in stark contrast to the one he tried to present to the LSAC. The unexpurgated version forms the plot for a cautionary tale that, in my view, should give pause to those who dismiss the potential for abuse in disability determinations. Because consultants who review documentation only see what the applicant submits, they usually can only wonder about the rest of the story. Does it make sense that the only report cards the applicant could locate were ones on which teachers voiced concerns? What were on the report cards he did *not* submit? Did anyone besides the examinee see him as distractible or impulsive? How is it that the clinician never bothered to explore whether factors other than those related to ADHD were at play? If you had a complete file of information, would the applicant come across as substantially impaired as compared to most people?

Students with bona fide problems supply that documentation with ease. Their file lays out a paper trail paved by report cards, past evaluations, score reports, and credible accounts by disinterested parties. In other cases, that path is not as well marked. The story of *Love* v. *LSAC* explains why a cautious attitude makes sense when evaluating the boundaries of that road less traveled.

CHAPTER 6

The Trial

The trial of *Love* v. *LSAC* commenced in Philadelphia on December 18, 2006, a total of 144 days after Mr. Charles Weiner filed the original complaint. The proceedings involved thirty-seven hours of testimony spread over five full days. Judge Surrick gaveled the court in session at roughly 9:15 every morning and sent us packing to our hotels around 7 PM every evening, except for the final day when the trial ended at 3:49 PM. Save for the one hour the judge allotted each day for lunch, the testimony and pleadings unfolded almost without interruption. He did allow for bathroom breaks along the way, but only a very few. Lady Justice may be blind, but she is apparently blessed with impressive bladder control.

The witnesses for the plaintiffs included Mr. Jonathan Love; his mother, Margaret Nader Love; AliceAnne Brunn, Ph.D., the clinician who evaluated the plaintiff in 2004; and M. Kay Runyan, Ph.D., an expert witness. The defense put on the stand Kim Dempsey, Ph.D., the LSAC's manager of accommodated testing; Charles Golden, Ph.D., an expert witness; and yours truly. Along with the lawyers and judge, these witnesses generated approximately 330,000 words of testimony recorded on over 2,200 pages of transcript.

One of the actors with a leading role in this legal drama left early in the week; Jonathan Love stayed only long enough to testify. By Tuesday afternoon he took leave of his own trial, for reasons that were never disclosed. According to his graduate school's course schedule, classes would have already ended for the semester. It is therefore unlikely he had to return because of academic responsibilities. It did not seem like he needed to return to Louisiana to see his mother given that she was in Philadelphia with him. Surely his attorneys would have offered the judge some compelling explanation had they one at hand. Where Jonathan Love had to travel was therefore left to the imagination. Regardless, his absence must have made Jonathan a far less sympathetic plaintiff in the court's eyes.

Another deponent who never appeared at trial was Dr. Hugh Van Auken, the psychologist from South Bend, Indiana who was the last to evaluate Mr. Love, in April 2006. He was the clinician who wrote the report reproduced in Chapter 1. Because it was Dr. Van Auken who actually completed the LSAC's professional verification form, his absence was conspicuous. Dr. Brunn had not seen Mr. Love since 2004, when he first applied for accommodations on the Graduate Management Admission Test (GMAT). Because she had not seen him since he was in college, Dr. Brunn was not in a position to give an opinion on Mr. Love's current status.

While it would seem that Dr. Van Auken's presence would be de rigueur, his absence was not a complete surprise. During his deposition, he had expressed the opinion that "it was a difficult argument to make that he [Jonathan Love] should receive accommodations" because his LSAT scores had been within normal limits without the benefit of accommodations. That, of course, was precisely the argument the LSAC was making in this case. I would have to think that Mr. Love's attorneys had no desire to have Dr. Van Auken voice that position in open court. It must have been sufficiently problematic for them that it was a part of the deposition transcript that the judge indicated he had read.

For those of us confined to Courtroom 8A for the duration, it was an exhausting week of early mornings, long days in court, and late nights of preparation for the next day. In my effort to keep this account focused more on fact than fancy, I will forego description of those moments that did not appear in the transcript: instances of adversarial irritations, humorous banterings, warm camaraderie, squirmy discomfiture, and charming displays of personal quirks. Suffice it to say that trials are intense, stressful, fatiguing, and exhilarating experiences. All the comparisons one hears between boxing matches and legal proceeding are apt. Like pugilism, trials require extensive preparation, anticipation of the opponent's strategies, quick thinking under duress, and awareness that one good punch can knock you to the canvas. The fate of combatants is also in the hands of judges with unfettered power to decide the match as they see fit. Even when the sparring centers on nuances of a federal disability law rather than jabs and right crosses, it is not an activity for the faint of heart.

Some inherent features of a trial are bound to raise blood pressure and galvanic skin response. The mere fact that absolutely everything is recorded creates an air of accountability and finality that can be daunting. All the players, the judge included, know that every word can come back to haunt you later on in this or future trials, on appeal, or if some medical school professor decides to write a book that uses the proceedings to illustrate certain diagnostic and legal issues. The tapping of the transcriber's keystrokes are a constant reminder that the courtroom is no place for imprecise language or loose statements.

Judicial demeanor is another element that ratchets up courtroom intensity. Most justices that I have observed behave just as Judge Surrick did for that week before Christmas. He sat there expressionless for all those hours, with just a glimmer of a smile when one of the attorneys made a joke or clever comment. Otherwise, he was inscrutable. It is always uncomfortable to interact with someone who withholds any feedback about what you have to say. You have this sense of flailing about, unsure if you are on the right track because the usual conversational guideposts are missing. And a judge is not just any participant in the dialogue. He is all powerful, the sole "decider." With just the words "sustained" or "over-ruled" he can gut your entire strategy, give you license to attack a person's credibility, disallow your best evidence, or make it easier to prove your case. That a participant with so much sway is mostly enigmatic makes for a charged atmosphere.

Because the judge is such a blank slate, courtroom conversations amongst lawyers seem to consist mainly of rampant guessing about his current mood, reactions, and state of mind. Judges become Rorschach cards draped in black robes. Any tidbit of judicial reaction becomes hyper-analyzed for its significance and meaning. I have seen supremely competent men and women with decades of courtroom experience dissolve into a morass of anxiety and depression based on a single question the judge asked a witness. Why would he ask that question? Do you think he didn't buy our argument? Oh my god, you don't think he agrees with the other side about that testing evidence, do you? Should we fly in another consultant to rebut that witness's response? Do you think we should re-work our closing? In the absence of clarity, anxiety takes hold.

Over the years, I have usually been more sanguine than most when the judge asks witnesses what might seem like troublesome questions. If I were a judge, I would do the same. It makes sense to test an argument by asking questions critical of that position, especially if I thought the lawyers missed opportunities to do so in their questioning. A state supreme court judge I met at a conference confirmed my suspicions. He told me that a judge's questions often fall in the devil's advocate genre. The strongest arguments are those that have been forged by the heat of probing questions and counterarguments.

The intensity of a trial also derives from the constant demand to think quickly on your feet. A witness or lawyer is not in a position to say, "Let me think about that question for a while and I'll get back to you." It all happens in the moment, with little space for reflection. The evening that follows a day of testimony offers generous chances to second-guess yourself. You find yourself thinking, "Why in the world didn't I come up with this response?" or "Boy, did I miss an opportunity to make a good point." Brilliance too often surfaces after the court's doors are closed for the day.

Before describing testimony that emerged over the week of trial, I want to highlight one brief episode that took place on the first afternoon. The lawyers for the LSAC consistently referred to ADHD as a mental illness or mental disorder. I imagine that they wanted to make the point that psychiatric disorders were not trifling matters, that they represented significant maladjustment. The following interchange, for me, captures the essence of the two mindsets at play in this trial. Ms. Leventhal is the attorney for the LSAC who is cross-examining Jonathan Love. Mr. Wolinsky is the lead counsel for the team handling the case for the plaintiff:

MS. LEVENTHAL:	As of the day of your deposition, other than not being able to stay attentive, and not being able to keep attention on one task, you couldn't think of another symptom of your mental illness, could you?
MR. LOVE:	I'm sorry?
MS. LEVENTHAL:	You couldn't think of any other symptoms of the mental illness that you've had for six years other than saying that you couldn't stay attentive or keep attention on a task. Is that fair to say?
MR. WOLINSKY:	Objection, Your Honor, this is the fourth time, I don't want to interrupt, but this is the fourth time counsel has referred to this as a mental illness, which it isn't.
THE JUDGE:	You are continuing to refer to it –
MS. LEVENTHAL:	It is.
THE JUDGE:	As a mental illness.
MS. LEVENTHAL:	It is a mental illness, I'm sorry that counsel is uncomfortable with that characterization, but it is. I can call it a lot of different things. It is a psychological disorder, it is a mental disorder, it is also a mental illness.
MR. WOLINSKY:	That is precisely the problem, Your Honor that people treat it as a mental illness, but this is a psychological diagnosis, and is not a mental illness.
MS. LEVENTHAL:	It is a mental illness.
THE JUDGE:	Counsel we will let you refer to it however you wish.
MS. LEVENTHAL:	Thank you.

I was in a courtroom years earlier when a similar moment occurred. It was during the hearing for the case of *Price* v. *National Board of Medical Examiners* (described in Chapter 4). A prominent national expert on ADHD was on the stand testifying about the process by which the diagnostic criteria were developed. He kept referring to ADHD as a psychiatric or mental disorder that had a detrimental affect on normal adjustment. The first time he used one of those terms, I could see the three medical students who had brought the action look at one another in obvious distress. One of them said something to their lawyer who, like Mr. Wolinksy, objected to the use of the term "mental disorder." The expert responded that it was indeed a mental disorder listed in the "Diagnostic and Statistical Manual of *Mental* Disorders" (the DSM-IV). He elaborated that ADHD met all the criteria for what constituted a disorder, primarily because it causes a person "harmful dysfunction."

From my perspective, Mr. Wolinsky's objection to use of the words "mental disorder" or "mental illness" reflects how he and other advocates want to both have and eat their piece of cake. Mr. Love's clinicians and attorneys worked to portray him as sufficiently disabled to warrant accommodations under the Americans with Disabilities Act. But they did not want to make him seem so impaired that he could not fulfill his responsibilities as an attorney. That depiction could have consequences for him when he went to gain admission to the bar or apply for jobs. Applicants for accommodations can therefore find themselves damned if they manifest insufficient impairment, but also damned if their impairments are substantial (or they present them as such).

The quandary is even more apparent for a medical student seeking accommodations. A state licensing board could conceivably refuse to grant a medical license to someone who was described as intensely distractible and impulsive. Many of us would prefer that these boards protect us from an anesthesiologist, for example, who reported a lifelong history of severe inattention. A job that requires someone to spend hours concentrating on meters and gauges may not be best filled by an individual who claims to have trouble sitting for more than ten minutes. And remember that physicians' medical licenses are unrestricted; they are given authorization to practice in whatever area they might choose.

This catch 22-type of bind arises all over the disabilities landscape. An individual has to be impaired enough to qualify as disabled but not so impaired that he is unable to perform the "essential functions of the job." Another example: An ADHD diagnosis can disqualify an individual from military service, especially if that person's treatment has included the prescription of stimulant medication. While it is ironic that someone who needs stimulants to maintain self-control might stop taking them so he can join the army and carry a gun, the regulations guiding recruitment are clear. The same for the guidelines relative to becoming a pilot: People with ADHD will find themselves restricted from receiving the medical certification necessary to obtain a license. Therefore, a student using an ADHD diagnosis to gain an accommodation on a standardized test may not realize the potential long-term implications of that request.

Fair or not, having a psychiatric diagnosis could conceivably affect eligibility for health insurance, employability, opportunities for gun ownership, and automobile insurance rates. While individuals like Jonathan Love would prefer to limit the impact of having an ADHD diagnosis to the granting of test accommodations, the reality may be otherwise. It is indeed a mental disorder that, by definition, causes global impairment. As data mount on its costs both to the individual and to society at large, students will have to accept that having an ADHD diagnosis may be more than a ticket to a prescription for stimulants or extra time on an examination. It can have unintended consequences.

The first morning of Jonathan Love's trial was devoted to opening statements. Mr. Wolinsky was the first to lay out his case for the judge. His remarks followed the logic of the original complaint closely. He quickly asserted what I have come to think of as the "What's the Big Deal?" argument. He told the judge that the LSAC was denying Mr. Love reasonable accommodations that would cost them little to grant:

> What he is asking for is routinely granted, and often granted, and that's time and a half for Jonathan, who through no fault of his own, reads with painful slowness. This case is all about those extra minutes, and the time to show his true abilities. It is a pretty modest request. He's not asking for a $10,000 ramp, he's not asking for a $75,000 elevator, he is not asking for a nickel's worth of damages, even though he might have. He's not asking for an injunction halting anything. LSAC, a $20,000,000 institution, has brought its enormous resources to bear just to keep Jonathan from getting this extra time.

Mr. Wolinsky is making the argument that most of us would pose if we were advocating for a Mr. Love. We would want the judge to think, "Why all of this fuss over a little extra time? Would the sun not rise in the morning even if he were to be granted those additional fifteen minutes per section?" In my view, a perennial challenge for the defense is to convince the judge that it is indeed a big deal. More time on a high-stakes exam means more time to complete more items. For someone who is not disabled, extra time constitutes an advantage. Aside from being unfair to other test takers, time accommodations for the undeserving warps a speeded test's ability to predict future performance. In the case of the LSAT, the deleterious impact of extra time on validity already has been documented.

After asserting that the ADHD and reading disorder diagnoses assigned to Mr. Love were fully substantiated, Mr. Wolinsky points to the plaintiff's two administrations of the GMAT as proof both of his disability and the ameliorative effects of extra time:

> But, the critical evidentiary factor here is Jonathan's very substantial score increase between the time he took the test unaccommodated, and he took it unaccommodated. He leaped, with one test in between, he leaped from the forty-fourth percentile to the eighty-eighth percentile, when he got accommodations and enough time to take the exam. Now this would be unheard of for a person who doesn't have a disability. It is very important evidence on two things. Number one, that he has the impairment, and secondly, that if he is given a little extra time, that accommodations help him to overcome that impairment.

Mr. Wolinsky argues that the fact that Jonathan Love's score improved with extra time verifies he has the impairment. According to his stance, only someone with a disability would have a higher score with more time. But is that true? Well, again, if a test is designed such that a person would not normally complete the items in the allotted time (which is the case for both the GMAT and LSAT), extra time would help almost anyone get a higher score. The only examinee whose score would not improve would be someone who was able to complete and check all the items within the standard time.

The general benefit of extra time for all test takers represents, for some, proof that it is not a fair or legitimate form of accommodation. The argument is that an accommodation should reduce the impact of the specific disability rather than represent a general advantage. For instance, a Braille version of the test, while it would help an examinee who was blind, would be of no benefit to test takers with normal vision. The same could be said for wheelchair ramps, handicapped accessible bathrooms, and sign-language interpreters. Although these accommodations allow individuals with handicapping conditions to perform on jobs or tests they could otherwise manage were it not for task-irrelevant limitations, they have no impact on non-disabled individuals. Indeed, an accommodation such as administering the test in Braille would actually reduce test scores for normally-sighted individuals.

According to this view, if extra time helps everyone taking a test, it must be that test-taking speed is essential to test performance, regardless of disability status. Contrast the general benefit of extra time to the impact of increasing the exam's font size. Because that accommodation would only help someone with limited vision, it must be that type size is generally irrelevant to what the test is designed to evaluate. If you printed a version of the LSAT in 42-point type, someone without vision problems would still get the same score. The LSAT is not a vision test; it is a measure of cognitive and academic skills. Therefore, it is fair to give someone with bona fide vision deficits a large-type version because that accommodation helps the person in ways that are irrelevant to what the test is intended to measure.

Some professionals advocate for a less stringent view of what represents a fair accommodation. They contend that an accommodation is reasonable if it helps someone with a disability significantly more than others. Evidence of what has been termed a "differential boost" for the disabled individual would justify the accommodation. An analogy could be made to a handicapped parking space; all customers would have a quicker walk into the store if they started from a closer spot. But parking space proximity would be of substantially greater benefit to someone who could barely walk.

A parallel to test-taking is harder to conjure. One scenario might involve a diabetic who needed time away from the test for insulin injections. While the opportunity to take breaks from a lengthy exam to stretch and take a deep breath might help anyone perform better, it would be of much greater benefit to the person with diabetes. The benefit of his "differential boost" could be dramatic if the accommodation helped him avoid lapsing into a diabetic coma. I imagine that most test takers would not object to that accommodation, even though it could be of general benefit.

The research on differential boost is somewhat inconclusive because results depend so heavily on the nature of both the test and test taker. Two of the earlier studies on the impact of extra time on learning disabled college students were actually conducted by Dr. M. Kay Runyan, an expert witness for the plaintiff. In the first study, published in 1991, Dr. Runyan selected thirty-one college students, sixteen of whom were identified as having a learning disability. All students were individually administered the Reading Comprehension subtest of the Nelson-Denny Reading Test, but were not told of a specific time limit. They were just asked to mark the test booklet when they were signaled that twenty minutes (the normal time for administration) had elapsed. They also could not return to the questions they had completed prior to the twenty minute interval.

Dr. Runyan reported that the non-learning disabled students performed better than the learning disabled students under the timed condition. However, those normally-achieving students, unlike their learning disabled counterparts, did not fare better with extra time. In fact, the scores of the LD students improved with extra time to such an extent that they had scores equal to what the non-LD students earned both under timed and untimed conditions. In the article and on the witness stand in Philadelphia, Dr. Runyan proclaimed these results (and similar findings from the second study) as documenting a differential boost of extra time for learning disabled students.

But are her data as compelling as she and others have claimed? For most researchers, those conclusions are not nearly so persuasive. Aside from identifying a range of methodological flaws, critics have highlighted one that is fundamental. It turns out that about half of the non-LD students finished the test in the twenty-minute window. They did not need the extra time because they were already done. The additional minutes were especially irrelevant because the instructions precluded them from working on the items they had completed in the first twenty minutes. Therefore, the design of the study allowed for "ceiling effects" that made it impossible to draw meaningful conclusions. A fair test of the differential boost hypothesis would have been to use a test even non-LD students could not have finished by the twenty-minute mark. With that study design Dr. Runyan could have explored whether the extra time would have helped non-LD students complete the unfinished items.

Some advocates dismiss such criticism of these Runyan-type studies. From their vantage point, the mere fact the extra time helped LD students normalize their scores is justification enough for extended time accommodations. And they would be right if the goal of an accommodation were to maximize outcome. If the Americans with Disabilities Act read, "People with disabilities should be accommodated on tests until such point that they can earn their best possible score or a score at least as high as most people," extra time for LD students would be sanctioned. But, of course, that is not the language of the ADA, nor does it make much sense to me. If the goal is for people with disabilities to perform optimally, why not just provide them with the answers to the exam?

Other research studies provide evidence that extra time helps normally achieving students *more* than it does those with a learning problem or ADHD. Ironically, such data suggest a form of reverse differential boost in favor of the non-disabled students. For example, a student, Ms. Cynthia Rogers, replicated Dr. Runyan's study design, but controlled for ceiling effects. She administered the Nelson-Denny to sixty-four high school students, half of whom had documented reading disabilities. Although the standard time for administration was set at 13 minutes, the students were asked to mark their progress at 6.5 minutes and at 19.5 minutes (the extended time phase). The results ran opposite to what Dr. Runyan found, most likely because the test had enough items for students to work on during the extra time. The students with learning disabilities had lower scores at each time interval. While they showed significant improvement with extended time, it was the non-learning disabled students who most benefited from the time extension.

Another former student, Dr. Roseanne Parolin, found similar results with ADHD middle school students to whom she administered a speeded/timed math test. The ADHD students performed more poorly than the non-ADHD students at each time interval. As with Ms. Rogers' study, the typical students were the ones who derived the greatest benefit from extra time. Contrary to Dr. Runyan's claims, extra time differentially boosted the fortunes of students without disabilities.

Unfortunately, no one has published a research study that examines the impact of extra time on the test performance of college students with ADHD. Without data, we are all left to rely on speculation and personal opinion. For what it is worth, however, most of us who work with students with ADHD would be surprised if data were to show that extra time helped the majority of them. ADHD is not a disorder that makes people move too slowly. Au contraire. Individuals with the disorder tend not to use the time they have wisely. They are so impulsive and distractible that they will not stay with a task long enough to complete it well. You will not find too many of these students re-focusing themselves over the course of the extended time. They would be long gone from the exam room, physically or otherwise.

The only study I know of that speaks to this issue is one I conducted with Dr. Kevin Murphy. The project involved adults who had come for an ADHD evaluation or had been solicited to serve in a research control group. The participants were assigned to either an ADHD group (because they met diagnostic criteria); a group of patients who met criteria for another psychiatric disorder or were not assigned a diagnosis at all; or a group of normal controls.

The finding that most grabbed our attention was that the majority of individuals with ADHD said they generally finished tests in the time allotted. In fact, more than a third of the group indicated that they completed tests ahead of time. Therefore, not all patients with this disorder perceive themselves as having been short on time when taking exams. The degree to which individuals in the ADHD group felt that they could have taken advantage of extra time depended on the test format: Half of the group felt that it would have helped to have extra time on multiple choice tasks. Yet more than two thirds said additional time would benefit them most for essay exams. This finding was intriguing in that most students request accommodations for standardized, multiple-choice tests, not for those involving extended written responses.

Perhaps the most intriguing results concern the responses of the normal control group. Forty-four percent had the impression that they usually finished *after* other examinees. Moreover, 34 percent felt they would have benefited from extra time on multiple choice tests and 64 percent could have used the extra time on essay exams (roughly the same percentages as the two psychiatric groups). What makes these findings interesting is that they highlight the extent to which normal individuals consider extended time as helpful for achieving better scores. The *perception* that extra time is helpful is therefore not unique to individuals with ADHD.

Parenthetically, some of the data from this study suggests that Mr. Love, were he to have had ADHD, would be better off requesting a room with reduced distractions. Fifty-six percent of the ADHD group answered affirmatively to the question, "Did you get so distracted when taking exams that you had trouble finishing them on time?" Far fewer in the two other groups answered this question in the affirmative. Sixty-one percent of the ADHD group said that it would have helped to have been tested in a distraction-reduced room compared to a much smaller percentage of the other groups. According to our data, individuals with ADHD more than others perceived a quiet testing room as helpful.

Last summer I heard anecdotal confirmation of what it might be like for someone with ADHD to handle timed examinations when I met a thirty-something fellow at a golf driving range. We were chatting about our jobs when the topic turned to my work around test accommodations. I explained that some individuals who claimed to have ADHD wanted extra time. He blurted out, "Well, that's dumb" and then told me his story: He had been diagnosed when he was seven with ADHD by one of our local psychologists and was eventually prescribed medication by his pediatrician. The rest of his tale involved special education services, a host of problems getting along with others, and an early exit from high school. After earning his GED, he tried attending one of our local community colleges, but without success. According to him, test-taking was his downfall, not because he did not know the material, but because he rushed through exams. He told me, "You could have given me triple time and it wouldn't have made a difference. I didn't even stay for the time they gave us. I'd just walk out thinking that I did great and I'd get the results back and find out I failed." His account is what clinicians like me tend to hear from our patients with true-blue ADHD, at least of the "Combined Type" that Jonathan Love claimed on his application for accommodations. Extra time to complete an exam probably just gives students with ADHD more opportunity to be restless, inattentive, and impatient.

In his opening statement, Mr. Wolinsky focused on Mr. Love's purported reading problems. He criticized the LSAC for over-focusing on ADHD although, in reality, the examinee never checked that box on the application for accommodations:

> Jonathan's impairment is in reading. His disability is manifested through slow reading speed, distractibility, and deficits in his ability to process written information quickly. Jonathan's impairment is caused by both learning disability and Attention Deficit Hyperactivity Disorder, ADHD. The evidence will show that defendants have mistakenly focused, almost exclusively, on ADHD, and practically ignored his learning disabilities. But, Jonathan has both. There are many types of learning disabilities. For example, most people read automatically and efficiently, and they process information that way. Someone with a learning disability of the type that Jonathan has takes longer to process written information, and read slower; ADHD can also greatly impact reading. The evidence will show that ADHD affects concentration, so that a person with ADHD may take longer to process written text, because they have difficulty concentrating on the written words.

To his credit, Mr. Wolinsky presented ADHD as distinct from a learning disability. People often (and erroneously) lump ADHD with learning disabilities and developmental disorders. While having ADHD unquestionably has a negative impact on academic functioning, it is not a learning disability, per se. The latter category refers to individuals who, because of some central neuropsychological deficit, cannot handle reading or math as well as most others. A student with a reading disability, for example, cannot read normally whether he is paying attention or not. His brain is simply not wired for reading. If the student with ADHD has problems reading, it would more likely stem from not concentrating sufficiently on the assignment. Unless he also had a learning disability, his success would depend more on whether he actually did the reading assignment rather on whether he had sufficient ability to read.

What about Mr. Wolinsky's claim that ADHD causes problems with reading? Is it clear-cut that those symptoms impair the ability to read quickly and with understanding? Alas, here we have yet another instance of a generally-accepted "fact" that has remarkably little support. Of the few studies that address the topic empirically, the results are a challenge to interpret. Even those studies that demonstrate reading deficits in children with ADHD describe the effects as "subtle." If students with ADHD have reading problems due to their ADHD (and not to having a specific learning disability), research has yet to unearth the link.

The most compelling data on the impact of ADHD on reading derives from a technology so new that we are just now writing up the results for publication. In collaboration with Dr. Lewandowski, my colleague from Syracuse University, and a software developer extraordinaire, Joshua Gordon, I have helped develop what we think is an ideal method for assessing test-related reading skills. It is based on what has proven to be one of Dr. Lewandowski's better ideas. A computer program we call TestTracker presents students with a multiple choice test in the same format as an SAT or ACT exam. The computer gathers extensive data on the student's vocabulary, reading speed, reading comprehension, and navigational strategy. It also administers questionnaires regarding test anxiety and personal perceptions of test-taking and reading skills. With one of our students, Ms. Rebecca Gathje, we tested 202 college students, of whom 35 had been professionally diagnosed with ADHD and had been approved to receive accommodations at the post-secondary level. They were comparable to the students in the control group on age, years in school, ethnicity, and verbal SAT.

The results of this study have been striking. On every measure of test performance, the students who had been professionally diagnosed with ADHD performed comparably to the other students. No differences emerged in reading speed or the number of correct items on measures of comprehension, vocabulary, and decoding. The two groups were also similar on a host of other performance indicators. Therefore, data from this sophisticated methodology failed to show reading deficits in a carefully selected sample of college students who had been identified as having ADHD.

Other data from this study confirmed what some of us consultant-types had suspected for years. Because so many of the examinees who request accommodations for medical board exams, bar examinations, and other professional certifications have achieved well in academic environments, one cannot help but wonder whether they may be more nervous than globally impaired. In many instances, their problems concentrating seem largely circumscribed to when they take high stakes examinations. Their accounts of sweaty palms, feeling overwhelmed, and being short of breath sound much more like signs of test anxiety than of a psychiatric disorder. Judge for yourself from this applicant's personal statement on an accommodations request: "The anxiety that accompanies taking an exam causes me extreme distraction and stress ... The pressure of the clock puts me into a panic and disables me from being able to process information and answer appropriately." Notwithstanding this description, the clinician attributed this applicant's poor concentration to "the stress of having ADHD" when other possible explanations presented themselves.

In her declaration, Mrs. Margaret Love described her son as showing just these kinds of test-related problems. Whenever he took such tests "he felt he was under a lot of pressure and would become very stressed and anxious." Even on practice tests he would "get anxious and have trouble concentrating" to the point that he would "shut down." As I pointed out in my declaration, these are clearly the reactions of an individual whose test anxiety may be substantial.

Our TestTracker-generated data lend some credence to the notion that at least some who request accommodations do so because they are anxious test-takers. While the students who had been diagnosed as ADHD performed as well as the control group on reading-based measures, they did diverge on other dimensions. The most significant differences were on a measure of test anxiety and another that asks students about perceptions of their reading and test-taking abilities. The students classified as ADHD were a much more anxious group even though they were equally capable.

In Mr. Love's case, none of the clinicians appeared to pursue the test anxiety angle. When Dr. Brunn was asked about this possibility during the trial, she demurred:

Q. And did you administer any tests to assess anxiety?
A. No, I did not.
Q. Why not?
A. I didn't feel that it was necessary.
Q. And why is that?
A. Because he didn't demonstrate symptoms of anxiety when I was observing him. He demonstrated a little initial nervousness, which is normal, and as I worked with him further I saw ADD symptoms, but I didn't see symptoms of anxiety or depression.
Q. Did Jonathan report at all getting nervous around test taking?
A. Yes. I believe that he did. He became nervous because he was concerned that he wouldn't be able to finish.
Q. And in your opinion, was there anything that leads you to believe that Jonathan's nervousness rises to the level of clinically significant anxiety or test anxiety?
A. No.

Why clinicians who submit documentation rarely pursue test anxiety as a potential explanation for test-related inattention is curious to me. It is a problem that is relatively easy to identify and treat. The payback to the test-anxious student can be quick and substantial in terms of improved exam scores. In fact, the benefit would likely outstrip the impact of extra time for most students. It strikes me as unfortunate that some clinicians are more eager to lock onto a clinical diagnosis than explore non-psychiatric factors that may be contributing to any test-related limitations.

In his opening and the questions of his experts that followed, Mr. Wolinsky made much of a link between a person's processing speed and ADHD. The plaintiffs, like many others advocating for accommodations, contended that: 1) slow processing speed is inherent in individuals with ADHD; and 2) additional testing time helps correct for that slowness. In Mr. Love's case, his processing speed was indeed his lowest index score on the intelligence test he took that Dr. Brunn administered to him in 2004.

First, for the link between ADHD and processing speed: Has research documented that connection? Are individuals with ADHD uniquely prone to perform poorly on measures of processing speed? Before drawing the bottom line on that literature, let me first explain how psychologists have generally defined that construct. The idea is that people differ on how quickly and efficiently they perform simple cognitive tasks. The assumption has been that people with learning problems and ADHD have slower rates of information processing that leave them in need of more time to complete tasks. The easiest analogy is to the speed at which computer chips process information: A computer with a slow processor will require more time to run applications.

As usual, the devil resides in the details of definition and measurement. While the benchmark for assessing computer clock speed has been well established, psychologists have not agreed upon a standard for assessing the human counterpart. They have used all manner of paradigms, from reaction-type measures to tests that require more information processing. The most popular method (and the one most in question at Jonathan Love's trial) is also relatively new on the diagnostic scene. It represents an index from the standard measure of intelligence, the Wechsler Adult Intelligence Scale Third Revision (or WAIS-III), introduced in 1997. This "Processing Speed Index" or PSI is calculated from scores on two subtests that require quick handling of visually-oriented tasks. For example, the Digit Symbol subtest presents the subject with a key that matches digits with certain symbols. On the rest of the page are boxes with just the digits and an empty space below. The subject has a fixed amount of time to put the appropriate symbol in each box.

Data on the Processing Speed Index are scant, mainly because it takes years to amass research sufficient to draw firm conclusions about the utility of a test score. Validating a score or index is also time-consuming and complicated. First, you have to show that the index is reliable, that it consistently measures what it is intended to measure. You would not want a thermometer, for example, that gave a different reading even though the temperature was constant. A researcher has to trust that the measurement technique is dependable.

The next step is to demonstrate that the index is "sensitive" to the deficits of the patient group it is designed to identify. In this case, one would have to demonstrate that adults with ADHD consistently earned lower PSI scores than a normal control group. Put another way, the PSI score should accurately predict which subjects were in the ADHD group and which were controls. It would also help the cause if you could show that the WAIS-III measure of processing speed showed results similar to other measures considered by the field to tap into that dimension.

The last challenge is to document the PSI's "specificity" by addressing this question: "If someone gets a low score on the PSI, does that mean he's likely ADHD or could it also mean he has a learning disability, anxiety disorder, seizure disorder, and/or some other problem?" If the index is not specific to ADHD, it reflects more of a universal deficit in individuals with psychiatric or learning disorders rather than a marker for ADHD, per se. A non-specific index might be useful as a general detector of maladjustment, but it would not have much to offer the clinician pursuing a precise diagnosis.

Another component of a research relevant to the issue of test accommodations looks at the validity of the index for predicting who might benefit from extra time. This sort of study would start by gathering PSI scores from a group of students. The researchers would next administer a version of a high-stakes examination both under standard conditions and with extended time. If the PSI could predict who benefited from the extra time and who did not, it would lend credence to use of the index for making decisions regarding test accommodations.

If all the studies about the PSI were conclusive, Mr. Wolinsky could fairly tell the judge, "You honor, the situation here is straightforward. Jonathan Love scored poorly on a psychological test index that is only low in groups of individuals with ADHD. Furthermore, scientific data demonstrate irrefutably that patients with ADHD who perform poorly on the PSI are likely to benefit from extra time. Given that it is an index with proven reliability and validity, the PSI should be considered proof positive that Mr. Love warrants test accommodations."

I imagine the reader is not surprised to learn that the data are nowhere near the point where Mr. Wolinsky could credibly stake that claim. First, results of studies comparing PSI scores in ADHD and normal samples have produced mixed findings. Individuals with ADHD are not always prone to score poorly on this measure of processing speed. Second, while it may be that individuals with ADHD are somewhat more likely than other students to have low PSI scores, that fall-off is not at all unique to ADHD. Low scores on the PSI are endemic to groups with a wide range of neuropsychological and psychiatric problems, including those associated with traumatic brain injury, fine motor problems, learning disabilities, autism, anxiety, conduct disorder, and poor motivation. The data suggest that individuals who have almost any type of limitation that renders them easily distracted will have trouble performing well on these measures.

In his opening statement, Mr. Wolinsky told the judge:

> Defendants say ... that you have to look at the effect of the impairment on test taking ability. Well, Your Honor, it is hard to imagine an impairment that more directly affects performance on a tightly time-limited test, than a substantial deficit in reading and processing speed.

While you cannot blame anyone for presuming a link between processing speed and test performance, the evidence gathered to date fails to forge that relationship, perhaps because current measures of processing speed are inadequate. More importantly, processing speed measures do not predict who will benefit from extra testing time. Indeed, the field has yet to develop a measure that provides that estimation with any degree of statistical confidence.

Another challenge for the plaintiff's legal team was to discount the diagnostic significance of Love's average LSAT score. In his opening statement, the attorney offered this explanation:

> The evidence will also show that Jonathan's average LSAT score, in the average range, reflects not only reasoning skills, but it reflects many pretest factors, such as rigorous studying, his hard work, preparatory classes, the use of practice exams, and so on. In addition, the LSAT average score is an outcome. The outcome says nothing, as the evidence will show, about the condition, manner, or duration of a disability, and that's the legal standard. So, the fact that a paraplegic might drag himself to the top of the stairs, that's the outcome. He got to the top of the stairs. According to LSAC, that shows that he doesn't have impairment, and therefore doesn't need a ramp, okay? As the court in Bartlett, which is cited in our brief, recognized the ADA does not focus on the final destination, but on the road travelled to arrive there ... Ultimately, to take the LSAT score, or any standardized test score, as the basis for deciding whether somebody gets an accommodation, asks the wrong legal question. The question is not whether he scored—the question isn't whether he is average, or better overall as a student, or average or better overall as a test taker. The legal issue is whether he is substantially impaired in a particular life function, okay?

Mr. Wolinsky first suggests that Jonathan Love achieved an average score on the LSAT because was able to practice. However, as the defense experts indicated in the trial (and I mentioned in the prior chapter), it would be impossible to achieve an average score on such an intensely complicated test merely by taking practice exams. While prep courses familiarize an examinee with the test's format, they do not cure severe reading disabilities. Nor can they review the exact content of items that will appear on a specific administration of the test; the list of potential topics for test items is limitless. If prep courses were as powerful as Mr. Wolinsky claimed, why would it be that, according to several reports, they boost an attendee's LSAT score by an average of only one or two points?

Mr. Wolinsky's comparison of Mr. Love's LSAT experience to a paraplegic pulling himself up the stairs represents another effort to defuse the impact of the fabled average score. As I understand it, he was arguing that the score could only be achieved at unusual cost to the examinee. Invoking the language of the EEOC regulations, Mr. Wolinsky said Jonathan Love was "significantly restricted as to the condition, manner, or duration under which an individual can perform a particular life activity as compared to the condition, manner, or duration under which the average person in the general population can perform the same major life activity." The problem, of course, is that it is not at all clear that Mr. Love's preparation or taking of the exam was any different in "condition, manner, or duration" than anyone else who took the exam. While he claimed he was unable to complete all the items, the fact is that most examinees fail to finish the test because that is how it is designed. No other evidence was introduced to document how Mr. Love's testing experience was any different from others in the room.

Mr. Wolinsky tried hard to link Dr. Brunn's observations of the plaintiff's behavior in her office with how he would likely perform on the LSAT. What follows is the segment of his cross-examination of Dr. Golden that addresses questions about how Mr. Love might have taken the test:

Q. Okay. You agree, do you not, that using a ruler or a piece of paper to hold a line, reading one word at a time, not skimming, mouthing words, having to reread paragraphs, getting fatigue, being distracted, this is not the way the average person reads, correct?

A. I would agree to that, except that if he really read that way, his score on the LSAT and the SAT would be much, much lower. And they don't allow you to bring in rulers and other things into the LSAT, the SAT, or the ACT examinations.

Q. Okay.

A. The problem with that whole description is he may have done that in front of her. I do not think Dr. Brunn is a liar or is making that up. But the reality is he couldn't have done that on the LSAT or the SAT, and if he needed to do that, he would have gotten scores near zero, the lowest scores possible on the LSAT, because he would have been unable to use such techniques in taking the test, and . . he would have read so slowly he couldn't have gotten through even a quarter or a fifth of the test.

During the "redirect" portion of Dr. Golden's testimony, Ms. Deon posed questions about the accommodations that Mr. Love did not request. If he was unable to take the test normally because of fatigue and distractibility, why did he not ask for accommodations that would have helped him with those limitations?

Q. Do you recall Mr. Wolinsky was asking you some questions about the manner in which Mr. Love took the LSAT, unaccommodated?

A. Yes.

Q. Okay. Do you recall that he was asking whether you knew that Mr. Love was fatigued, that he claims to have been fatigued during the taking of the LSAT?

A. Yes.

Q. Have you ever reviewed a request for accommodations that included a request for breaks in between the thirty-five minute sections?

A. Yes, we have had people with disorders who claim they get rapidly fatigued, ask for extended times between sections of the test, which at least I have suggested be granted.

Q. Did Mr. Love make that request in this matter?

A. No, he did not.

Q. How about the suggestion that you didn't know whether Mr. Love may have been distractible when he was taking the October of 2003 LSAT. Do you remember those questions?

A. Yes, I do.

Q. I would ask you, have you ever had a review of a request for accommodations where the individual claimed they were distractible, and needed an extra, or separate, room for taking the LSAT?

A. That's a frequent request.

Q. Okay. Would that be something that potentially would be related to attention issues?

A. Yes, absolutely.

Q. Was there such a request made in this matter?

A. No, there wasn't.

Q. Let me ask, even if those were—even if that was the case with Mr. Love, that he was fatigued or distracted while he was taking that October 2003, LSAT, would that have any bearing on the opinion that you have rendered?

A. Not in terms of giving him additional time, because again, if he really had those conditions and they were serious, his score would have been substantially lower than it actually was. So, even if he has these conditions, he somehow is able to overcome them, within the normal functioning of the test.

When I was asked about the "condition and manner" during the cross-examination, my response was uncomplicated but similar in spirit to what Dr. Golden had testified:

Q. You are really not able to make a comment, with respect to how Jonathan went about tackling, or the condition under which he took the LSAT, are you?

A. Well, I know the condition he took it was unaccommodated, so –

Q. Well, when I referred to his condition, the manner in which he went about taking the LSAT. You don't really know.

A. How he got his average score, I don't know.

Q. Okay. The only thing you are able to state with respect to Jonathan's unaccommodated LSAT score is that it was average. You can't say whether or not it accurately reflects his ability, can you?

A. I don't know how one judges what his ability would be.

Q. All right. You can only say that he scored within the average range, isn't that correct?

A. What I saw was that he scored in the average range, that's correct.

Another element of Mr. Wolinsky's strategy was to unlink test taking from the ADA's consideration of a major life activity. He said, "In addition, taking the LSAT, taking a standardized test of any kind, is not a major life activity, and the impairment in a major life activity is what's legally relevant." I have been baffled by this statement since the moment I heard it in Philadelphia. I cannot grasp why it made sense for Mr. Wolinsky to remove test taking from coverage by the ADA. If taking an exam is not closely associated with a major life activity, why were we in court? I thought the ADA was about providing accommodations to people who were unable to perform tasks associated with a major life activity? Is Mr. Wolinsky saying that someone who has been qualified as disabled should receive accommodations for any activity, regardless of the task in question?

The main thrust of the plaintiff's argument was that someone should be considered disabled if he has been diagnosed as such. A diagnosis, according to the plaintiff's attorneys, verifies what the ADA requires by way of a "substantial impairment in a major life activity." If the student's disorder might limit optimal performance, accommodations should be provided. From the DRA standpoint, the LSAC was discriminating against Mr. Love because they refused to let the ADHD diagnosis grease the way to extended testing time, even in the face of a solid performance on an untimed administration of the test. Indeed, Mr. Wolinsky argued that the LSAC "broke the rules" by, in his view, basing the accommodations denial entirely on the attainment of an average score.

Ms. Grace Deon, in her opening argument for the defense, told the judge that the average LSAT score was only one pixel in the canvas of Jonathan Love's impressive accomplishments. Presaging the testimony of Dr. Dempsey and the other experts, she laid out the evidence of the plaintiff's consistent competence. She explained that the LSAC declined the request because the documentation failed to show that he was substantially impaired. A snippet from her opening focuses on his normal childhood and successful college career:

> The evidence will reveal not only that Mr. Love is academically successful, but that he managed to succeed without any formal special education. Concerning his educational career prior to college, Mr. Love was never referred for a psychological evaluation. Even though Mr. Love was in a private school setting, no teacher, no guidance counselor, no principal, not his own family physician, or even his mother felt there was a need to refer him to be assessed for any type of psychological evaluation, due to ADHD-like symptoms, or reading difficulties, for that matter ... Plaintiff will tell you that he received a 3.1 GPA from Baylor University, while obtaining a dual degree in finance and business finance real estate. He will testify that he studied for and received his real estate license in the states of Texas and Louisiana. He took those tests without accommodations. They were timed tests, and there were no accommodations, although they are permissible and available by virtue of the ADA. Mr. Love will tell you that in an essay to the Notre Dame University MBA program, he described himself as adept at multitasking. Mr. Love will also tell you that his ability to focus on the task at hand is a lifestyle he has learned to live by. The extent of Mr. Love's ability to manage his daily life, educationally, socially, and vocationally is very evident, and is without any impairment.

Ms. Deon bolstered her oration by showing PowerPoint-type slides that reviewed Jonathan Love's record. She seemed intent on demonstrating to the judge that Love's was a life uncharacteristic of an individual with an impairing psychiatric or learning disorder. One such visual listed his high school activities, including some of his athletic (captain of both the varsity football and basketball teams; player on varsity baseball team, member of the soccer team) and academic achievements (honor roll; listing in *Who's Who Among American High School Students*; final grade point average of 3.1). That slide also illustrated his capacity to be highly involved in a range of extra-curricular, volunteer, and work activities. These included: Key Club, Loyola Ambassadors; Christian Life Community; Fellowship of Christian Athletes; reporter and photographer for the school newspaper; Flyers Aiding the Hungry; Veterans Administration Volunteer; Habitat for Humanity; St. Catherine's Youth Group; and St. Joseph's altar server.

What attracted the most attention during the trial was his years as a life-guard, especially the summer he served as head lifeguard. It seemed implausible that someone with attention deficits could have been competent at a job that was all about being attentive. Yet, according to the record, he performed well in that position.

The opening statement next highlighted the disconnect between diagnosis and disability. Ms. Deon proposed that a diagnosis does not alone demonstrate a substantial limitation:

> Even if plaintiff's records established a valid clinical diagnosis, this would not automatically entitle Mr. Love to these accommodations. Of utmost importance is that he establish that his ADHD and alleged difficulties with processing speed, that they substantially limit his ability to engage in major life functions. In the context of this analysis, that would be reading and learning.

While she indicated the need to show impairment in a major life activity, Ms. Deon chose not to narrow the focus to test taking, per se, perhaps because Mr. Wolinsky had charged that the LSAC over-relied on that LSAT score. Otherwise she might have cited the ADA-requirement for evidence that the disorder directly impacts the person's ability to accomplish the task at hand, in this instance, test taking. For example, a person could have a legitimate learning disability in math but not receive accommodations on a test of reading comprehension. Accommodations are only intended to ameliorate deficits that affect performance on a specific job or activity.

Later in the week, Dr. Charles Golden had no trouble making that impairment-to-task connection:

> Even if I accepted the diagnosis ... the disability has got to be related to the LSAT. I've got students who are paraplegics. They're in wheelchairs, but they don't need extra time. They have a disability, no question about it, but they don't get extra time on the LSAT. They may get a ramp into the room, but that's about it. They're not going to get extra time because they don't need extra time because their disability has nothing to do with it. I have students with major Asperger's Disorder. They are very bright, but have incredible social problems. Now, when they test in a room full of people ... they get very anxious being close to a lot of people. So they needed a quiet room, but they didn't need extra time. They had a clear cut disability, there was no question about it, but they just needed an extra room, a quiet room. They didn't need to have extra time. So having a disability or having a major life-impairment is not the definition by itself of whether or not you get extra time on the LSAT because what we're doing here is giving people an equal playing field. We're not giving someone an advantage.

Dr. Golden stated the case for denial about as straightforwardly as possible. How could Mr. Love be disabled in his ability to take a test if he can pass a test most people are not even in a position to take? And even if, by some statistical improbability, he was able to pass the LSAT despite a purported reading disorder, how can you dismiss an entire educational record that shouts normality?

In her testimony, Dr. Dempsey provided what to me was compelling evidence of Mr. Love's high level skills. When she was contrasting his performance on the relatively easier Nelson-Denny with his scores on the LSAT reading comprehension test, she showed a passage from the actual test that he took. Mr. Love answered correctly five of the six questions associated with the passage. Reprinted below is one section of the fifty-five line item:

> Copyright law outlines several factors involved in determining whether the use of copyrighted material is protected, including: whether it is for commercial or nonprofit purposes; the nature of the copyrighted work; the length and importance of the excerpt used in relation to the entire work; and the effect of its use on the work's potential market value. In bringing suit, the publishers held that other copy-shop owners would cease paying permission fees, causing the potential value of the copyrighted works of scholarship to diminish. Nonetheless, the court decided that this reasoning did not demonstrate the course packs would have a sufficiently adverse effect on the current or potential market of the copyrighted works or on the value of the copyrighted works themselves. The court instead ruled that since the copies were for educational purposes, the fact that the copy-shop owner had profited from making the course packs did not prevent him from seeking protection under the law. According to the court, the owner had not exploited copyrighted material because his fee was not based on the content of the works he copied; he charged by the page, regardless of whether the content was copyrighted.
>
> In the court's view, the business of producing and selling course packs is more properly seen as the exploitation of professional copying technologies and a result of the inability of academic parties to reproduce printed materials efficiently, not the exploitation of these copyrighted materials themselves. The court held that copyright laws do not prohibit professors and students, who may make copies for themselves, from using the photoreproduction services of a third party in order to obtain those same copies at a lesser cost.

To demonstrate Jonathan Love's strong reading comprehension skills, Dr. Dempsey presented data on the readability of that passage. The most common method of assessing readability is called the Flesch-Kincaid Readability Test. It uses a formula (that Microsoft Word's "spelling and grammar" module calculates automatically) based on word and sentence length; it generates an estimate of grade level and reading ease. The full version of the LSAT passage excerpted above had a grade level index of 22, or the equivalent of someone with ten years of education past high school. While I had been aware that the test was challenging, I did not realize that it required reading comprehension skills at that advanced level.

Mr. Love's obvious reading proficiency as reflected by his LSAT score was even more significant because it made his first percentile score on the Nelson-Denny Reading Test all the more implausible. The exhibit showed that one of the passages on that screening test he supposedly could not manage had a readability index at eighth grade. Dr. Golden was not at all hesitant to offer his characterization of Mr. Love's curiously low score: "It is one of the worse Nelson-Denny's I have ever seen in an individual who . . . has not been run over by a truck or something along those lines." The judge must have been impressed by Dr. Golden's view; as you will see, that reference to a truck accident was included in his final ruling.

Other interludes in the trial reflected the defense's efforts to normalize what the plaintiff's team sought to pathologize. One brief but telling interaction concerned characterizations of Mr. Love's forgetfulness. When asked during cross-examination how he could be so disorganized yet still manage the logistical demands of world travel, he and his mother made much of his absent-mindedness. Mrs. Love also said he was unusually scattered in his management of daily responsibility.

In her cross examination of Dr. Brunn, Ms. Leopold-Leventhal took the opportunity to reveal certain of the defense team's travel travails. Because of what is known as "work product confidentiality," I cannot reveal the name of the expert witness who forgot his pants. That would divulge the inner workings of the defense team. You should know, however, that Dr. Golden's pants seemed to match just fine and I was the only other male expert witness:

Q. There was a lot of testimony yesterday and today about things that Mr. Love forgets or misplaces or doesn't remember to bring from one place to another. When I arrived at my hotel on Sunday, my co-counsel told me that she forgot her contact lenses and her husband had to have them FederalExpressed to her. My legal counsel forgot her stockings and an earring. Unfortunately, one of my expert witnesses forgot a pair of pants. I didn't forget anything. Did you forget to bring anything with you on this trip, Dr. Brunn?

A. Yes. I did.

Q. What did you forget?

A. I forgot several things actually, but nothing that was of critical importance.

A similar moment occurred during my testimony when Ms. Deon asked me about my impressions of Jonathan Love's hours on the witness stand. It was an effective question because none of us could get over how calm, patient, and well-spoken he was as a witness, both at the deposition and trial. If you were to view the video of the deposition, for example, you would have been impressed by his composure. The lawyers even produced a trial exhibit that showed how long he sat at one stretch during the deposition.

> Q. Dr. Gordon, can you tell Judge Surrick and the court what you observed from a clinical standpoint that was of any significance to you during the time of Mr. Love's videotaped deposition?
> A. I thought how he handled his videotaped deposition and also here in court was very impressive. He thought before each question. Over the five hours he must have been here [testifying] plus however long he was in his deposition, he almost never interrupted. He clearly is a thoughtful fellow. He responds well and didn't move much at all. He seemed to handle it in a very straight forward way. Actually, I have to say that, out of all of us who testified, he seems the most reflective and the least likely to jump in when he is not supposed to.

During cross-examination, I was asked again about my impressions of Mr. Love:

> Q. I believe you had testified that Jonathan's behavior in court was not indicative of a person with ADHD, because he was reflective?
> A. I observed that. I was just kind of interested that somebody that was supposed to be that slow and plodding and inattentive and distractible sat here and handled this circumstance so well.
> Q. People who often like to think about information, and process that information, might be the type of person who might be slow, and prodding, and reflective, as you described.
> A. He was not plodding. When he was asked to go to a page [in the book of exhibits], he went to that page. I was trying to see if he was mouth reading like people said he had to in order to read. The only person I saw mouth reading was one of the lawyers involved. I didn't see it for him. If you asked him to go to a page, he turned to the page just as quickly as any of us have.

Having chomped at the bit all those hours in court, I was far more relieved at finally having a chance to speak my mind than I was anxious about testifying. Also, by that late point in the proceedings, exhaustion and an eagerness to head home for the holidays had taken hold. The atmosphere had become less solemn, more casual. But I was determined to debunk what I saw as two especially egregious statements by the plaintiff's experts. The first was by

Dr. Brunn, when Ms. Jennifer Weiser asked her about Mr. Love's performance on one of the psychological tests:

> Q. And you said that Jonathan's approach to this test is consistent with what you see in people with ADHD, is that correct?
> A. With certain types of ADHD. The type he has is the diligent type of ADHD, where he is the kind of person who has significant problems with attention and organization, but once he is able to sit down and focus and concentrate in an environment that's appropriately quiet, he is able to perform well, given enough time.

I remember leaning over to Ms. Leopold-Leventhal and asking, "Did she really say that?" It was hard for me to fathom that anyone could assert a "diligent type" of ADHD. If anything, ADHD is a disorder of diligence. All of the symptoms stand as roadblocks to someone being able to sustain effort over time. As I later explained it to the judge: "So this concept of ADHD diligent type is, that's like 'Paraplegia—Walking Type' or 'Blindness—Seeing Type' or 'Retardation—Intelligent Type.' It's just oxymoronic. It just can't be." I felt a whole lot better getting that off my chest.

I also wanted a chance to refute the notion offered by Drs. Runyan and Brunn that a child could have ADHD in such a way that no one at school would notice. When asked how it was that none of the teachers commented on report cards or to his mother about any behavior problems, they indicated that some children with ADHD showed their symptoms quietly. To anyone who has ever managed children with this disorder or studied the clinical research literature, that contention is entirely out of bounds with reality. ADHD is listed in the DSM-IV as a "Disruptive Behavior Disorder" for good reason. It is indeed disruptive to just about anyone who has to work with that child in circumstances that require attention and self-control. It was especially far-fetched in the case of someone that Dr. Runyan had characterized as "severely impaired" by the subtype of the disorder that included both inattention and hyperactive/impulsive behavior. The interchange during my direct examination went as follows:

> Q. I ask you, What is the possibility, if any, of other individuals not being able to recognize characteristics of someone with severe ADHD?
> A. Given the nature of the disorder, that would be like not recognizing that a child's hair was on fire or something that obvious.

I also wanted the judge to understand that the rationale Dr. Brunn gave for how Jonathan Love was able to manage being a lifeguard for so many years had no basis in research. She tried to explain away his obvious capacity to concentrate by invoking the "hyper-focus" canard so often used by clinicians who have to account for high-functioning in a supposedly impaired student. At trial she was asked what she meant when she said that Mr. Love was "hyper-vigilant":

Q. Well, what does hyper-vigilant mean?
A. That's when a person hyper-focuses to overcome their ADD.
Q. Do you have any reason to believe that the concept of hyper-vigilance is not linked to ADD, but it was actually first identified with respect to autistic children?
A. I'm sure it was possibly first identified there. But, I think that hyper-vigilance can exist in other situations, both related to ADD and related to nothing but being hyper-vigilant.
Q. And you base that on your clinical observations. No actual studies or no data from the field. Is that correct, Doctor?
A. Correct.

The simple fact is that individuals with ADHD have never been shown to have a capacity to hyper-focus. If someone can compensate successfully by concentrating that intently without medication or other extraordinary interventions, he likely does not meet criteria for an ADHD diagnosis. Hyper-focus and ADHD rings about as true a combination as acute hearing and deafness. As Ms. Deon's questions suggest, that symptom is far more associated with autism; such individuals find it hard to move their attention away from a narrow interest or preoccupation.

One other opportunity for myth-busting presented itself during my cross-examination. I knew it would arise because I saw the list of exhibits the plaintiffs had disclosed prior to the trial. Having spent time researching the topic, I was pleased I had the chance to respond. It centered on the plaintiff's effort to support the notion that highly accomplished individuals could legitimately be considered as having ADHD. Mr. Weiner, the lawyer who cross-examined me, showed a placard filled with familiar names of individuals, some well-known, who purportedly had learning disabilities and/or ADHD. When I researched their histories online, I found most had reported minor reading problems in elementary school. Anderson Cooper of CNN, for example, reported "mild dyslexia" and a tendency to speak too quickly. He nonetheless managed to achieve well enough to attend Yale University. A voice coach helped him speak slower.

I am not quite sure how Dr. Baruj Benacerraf, a winner of the 1980 Nobel Prize for Medicine, made it on the list. According to his autobiography he had excellent grades at Columbia University after having been schooled in Venezuela and France. Also on the poster was Richard Branson, the founder of Virgin Airways. It is hard to imagine he was too impaired given that he established a national magazine when he was sixteen, the "Student Advisory Centre" upon turning seventeen, and what became Virgin Records when he was twenty.

Mr. Weiner's tack was to ask my opinion about certain colleagues who had proclaimed themselves as having ADHD. He mentioned Drs. John Ratey and Ned Hallowell, two psychiatrists who collaborated on the popular book, "Driven to Distraction." I am afraid I might have become a bit slaphappy by this point in the trial:

Q. Well, aren't Dr. Ratey and Dr. Hallowell both medical doctors?
A. They are both medical doctors.
Q. They are both psychiatrists?
A. They're both psychiatrists.
Q. It would be adverse to your business interests, adverse to your medical interests as a practitioner, to say you have ADHD, don't you agree?
A. Do you really want me to answer that?
Q. Do you think that somebody who is a medical doctor, it would be appropriate for them to disclose that they have ADHD?
A. Dr. Hallowell first announced that he had ADHD when he was promoting "Driven to Distraction." He then wrote a book, and I can't remember the title of it, but it was about anxiety disorder. I heard him say that he also had an anxiety disorder. This led some of us to worry that his next book might be about male sexual dysfunction or schizophrenia.

Mr. Weiner nonetheless continued to elaborate on his list of celebrities who might have had learning problems or ADHD. He mentioned another psychologist, Dr. Kathleen Nadeau, and a lawyer who has apparently written about special education issues. His efforts ended after this interchange:

Q. There is a number of athletes who have been attributed with ADHD. Michael Jordan and . . .
A. Mr. Weiner, the world has ADHD right now. I think you could go on with your list until well into Christmas with all the people who either say they have ADHD or people who others presume have it. Some said Bill Clinton had ADHD, and that's why he had certain impulse control problems. He did okay for himself from a job performance point of view, though.

Near the end of my testimony (and therefore of the trial itself) I had an opportunity to tell the judge what had been on my mind from the moment I first read the documentation in July until my courtroom appearance on this day before Christmas. It was one of those simple, crystallizing thoughts that organizes an otherwise cluttered tableau. I expressed it in response to a question about my general impression of the documentation when I first received it from Dr. Dempsey:

> And now, all these months and four thousand pages later, I look at it all and say what I've said to myself all along: "This is somebody who is claiming ADHD as an impairment. But, essentially, his impairment is that he didn't get as high a score on the LSAT as he wanted to. And that's just not my idea of an impairment or disability."

Ms. Deon, in her opening statement, had sounded the same theme:

> In short, the entire lawsuit is about Mr. Love's sense of entitlement to receive an LSAT score that reflects him having additional time, and allowing him to perform to his full potential ... The Law School Admission Counsel is confident that, when this trial is over, Your Honor will conclude that Mr. Love has failed to meet his burden to prove and establish that he is disabled under the ADA. The ADA requires that the Law School Admission Counsel compare him to the average person. The evidence will demonstrate that, when doing so, he is not substantially limited. Defendant's witnesses will testify that such a result is not what the drafters of the ADA intended. In summary, contrary to plaintiff's position, equal footing under the ADA does not equate to test takers maximizing or reaching their full potential. Such a result is contrary to the law and inherently unjust.

And after the closing gavel sounded, we were all left to wonder whether the judge agreed.

CHAPTER 7

The Final Order

After months of demanding trial preparation, followed by five days of all-out exertions in and around Courtroom 8A, the sudden switch to standby mode was jarring. While my withdrawal symptoms never quite included delirium tremens, they nonetheless produced many an anxiety-tinged reverie: What if he actually ruled for the plaintiff despite what seemed like an airtight case against him? What would happen to the accommodations process if the judge thought Mr. Love was sufficiently impaired to warrant extra time? Is it possible that an MBA student at Notre Dame could be considered legally disabled by learning-related disorders?

Weeks elapsed without a word from the judge. While the wait was excruciating, Surrick's lack of urgency in issuing the ruling would seem to have boded well for the defense. Remember that the judge had expedited the trial so that Mr. Love's accommodated scores could be considered in the upcoming law school admissions cycle if the LSAC lost the case. As the vigil moved past February (when deadlines closed), it seemed that the ruling might not favor the plaintiff.

After several false alarms, the judge's clerk indicated that the order would be issued for certain on the morning of Friday, March 9, 2007, a total of seventy-seven days after the trial's end. That morning might not have been my most productive on record. For me, the suspense was of the sort usually reserved for wondering if the baby will be a boy or girl, the clock will elapse before the opposing team scores the winning touchdown, or that letter in your mailbox has good news about your grant application. As the hours passed, the suspense rose to incapacitating heights, ultimately rendering me incapable of doing much other than staring dumbly at my e-mail in-box and checking that my cell phone was active. By around four o'clock, certain I'd be spending another weekend in suspended agitation, I went shopping for dinner.

And then the call came from Ms. Leopold-Leventhal. The fax from Judge Surrick's clerk had arrived. The LSAC had won the case, big time. Mr. Jonathan Love was not entitled to extended time on the LSAT.

While I will describe the "Findings of Fact, Conclusions of Law & Order" in some detail, you can review it for yourself online at: http://www.paed. uscourts.gov/documents/opinions/07d0299p.pdf. You can also find on the Web and in the Resources section the many other related cases I discuss in this chapter.

If you have never read a complete legal opinion, it is a worthwhile exercise. You might be surprised, as I have been, by how many details judges include about the case at hand. A lawsuit might end up establishing a broad legal precedent, but it all begins with a story, often about someone like you or me. Reading that story can draw you into cases that might otherwise seem mundane or technical. It is one reason I chose not to fictionalize the story of the Love trial. A description based on anything other than real-life events would have surely detracted from the immediacy and credibility of the account.

A quick example of how celebrated cases emerge from quotidian events: Earlier I mentioned an ADA-related case on which the Supreme Court issued an opinion in 1997. The ruling in *Sutton* v. *United Airlines* was central in establishing the principle that an individual is not legally disabled under the ADA if "corrective measures" allow for normal functioning. That precedent emerged from a commonplace hiring issue. Identical twins, Karen Sutton and Kimberly Hinton, had applied for pilot positions with United Air Lines. Although both had extensive experience flying commuter planes for regional airlines, they shared a "life long goal to fly for a major air carrier."

In 1992, the sisters were invited to interview for United Airlines. Unfortunately, they were informed at the interview that their uncorrected vision disqualified them from pilot positions with United; the company's policy required pilots to have uncorrected vision of 20/100 or better in each eye. The plaintiffs' uncorrected vision of 20/200 in the right eye and 20/400 in the left eye disqualified them for the position even though their eyesight was 20/20 with glasses or contact lenses. The sisters filed a lawsuit in federal court pursuant to the Americans with Disabilities Act, likely unaware that their effort to seek employment would end in a Supreme Court ruling with

widespread repercussions for disability law. While cases may become prece-
dential, they evolve from particulars of the commonplace.

If you read the opinion in the matter of *Jonathan Love* v. *the Law School
Admission Council*, you will find where I have been drawing much of the information I have written about in this book. The amount of detail is extensive. It reviews Mr. Love's entire academic career, including teacher
comments from his elementary school report cards, the grades he received
in his high school, all of his scores on each administration of his college entrance examinations, and which teachers allowed him and other students to
have extra time on tests. It lists the name of the gallery his mother owns
and the books he had to read for one high school English class. The opinion even describes his athletic record:

> He was the starting fullback on offense, the starting outside linebacker on
> defense, and was on both the punting team and the kickoff team in his senior
> year. He also played on his high school's baseball team where he was the start-
> ing center fielder. Plaintiff's participation in athletics required that he memo-
> rize as many as twenty different offensive plays in football and a number of
> hand-signals in baseball. As a result of Plaintiff's athletic skills in both football
> and baseball, he was on the field almost the entire game which required him
> to focus and perform specific tasks. His talents, particularly in football, won
> him the "All District Honorable Mention Award" during his senior year of
> high school.

The credibility issues I wrote about in Chapter 4 are fully described in
the opinion, from the discrepancies in Mr. Love's account of his work history at Nader's Gallery to the questions around who, if anyone, prescribed
him stimulant medication. The judge also detailed what Drs. Brunn and
Van Auken did not know about Jonathan Love because they accepted what
he and his mother reported at face value. For example, the opinion pointed
out some of the realities lost on Dr. Brunn when she wrote her report:

> When Dr. Brunn authored her report, she was not aware of the fact that Plain-
> tiff's elementary school grades and IOWA Reading test scores were all within
> the average range. She did not know that he studied for and passed the Texas
> and Louisiana real estate licensing exams in the fall of 2004 without accommo-
> dation. She did not know that Plaintiff sat for a full day of interviews with two
> brokerage houses and received job offers as a result of those interviews. She did
> not know that he served as a teaching assistant for a graduate course in entre-
> preneurship in the West Indies during the summer of 2006. Dr. Brunn admit-
> ted that she relied upon self-reports that Plaintiff's uncle had been diagnosed
> with ADHD. In fact, Plaintiff's uncle has not been formally diagnosed with
> ADHD.

The judge described other "problems with relying on self-reporting to make an assessment" that reflected errors more of commission than omission:

> Plaintiff's psychologists relied on self-reporting as well as clinical observation in reaching their conclusions. In this regard, there is some question as to the reliability of some of the information provided. The evidence in this case concerning the prescribing and use of the medication Adderall is perplexing. Moreover, the testimony concerning Plaintiff's application to graduate school demonstrates a willingness to exaggerate to the point of misrepresentation.

The reader will remember that at issue in the trial was the legitimacy of certain test scores, particularly on the Nelson-Denny Reading Test. The clinicians had pointed to Mr. Love's extremely low score as evidence of a learning disability. The experts for the LSAC argued that these scores were of dubious validity given his performance on other tests, his solid score on the LSAT, and his overall academic attainment. In one brief footnote, the judge dismissed the Nelson-Denny scores when he wrote: "We give little credence to Plaintiff's scores on the NDRT. They are so low that they must be treated as outliers or worse." Those last two words would seem to indicate that the Judge shared the defense's opinion that the outlier data might more reflect Mr. Love's desire to gain accommodations than an actual deficit in reading speed. He even cited Dr. Golden's statement that those first percentile scores were the worst he had ever seen in an individual "who has not been run over by a truck or something along those lines."

In taking the clinicians to task for their failure to gather evidence beyond self-report, Judge Surrick delivered a clear message to mental health professionals: If you are going to evaluate whether an individual falls under the protection of the Americans with Disabilities Act, you had better get your facts right. Furthermore, getting those facts right means not relying entirely on the account of someone who has a vested interest in a specific outcome. If the case of *Love* v. *LSAC* demonstrates anything, it is that a valid disability determination cannot hinge on unsubstantiated self-report. Mr. Love is surely not the only student whose desire to "do much better and get into a very good law school" trumps a willingness to provide the unvarnished truth. Like it or not, clinicians must insist on receiving from their clients external evidence to substantiate personal anecdote.

The judge's opinion supports other principles of clinical assessment that the defense experts strove to establish. He agreed in no uncertain terms that determination of diagnostic (and disability) status is not simply a matter of producing a few abnormal scores from psychological testing. It is not that the judge dismissed psychological testing altogether but more that he considered those results within the context of Mr. Love's actual functioning. By dismissing the notion that psychological tests can somehow divine a disorder (other than retardation) in isolation, Judge Surrick added his voice to the chorus of other judges who expect evidence of functional impairment to extend beyond the posting of a test score.

Judge Surrick's opinion comes to a crescendo when he ties *Love* v. *LSAC* to two prior decisions involving the National Board of Medical Examiners (NMBE). I described both cases ("Price" and "Gonzales") in earlier chapters. He singled out the Gonzales case as particularly relevant:

> In *Gonzales*, the plaintiff sought an accommodation for the medical boards because he had a disability related to slowness in language processing. Gonzales graduated from high school, received a 1050 (out of 1600) on the SAT without an accommodation, graduated from the University of California at Davis with a 3.15 GPA, took the MCAT twice, and was accepted at the University of Michigan Medical School. Gonzales had no history of formal accommodations prior to asking for one on the medical boards. As the *Gonzales* Court noted, "[a]lthough significant academic achievement does not negate a student's claim that he has a learning disability, the education history is relevant to the inquiry." The court in *Gonzales* was persuaded by testimony that the plaintiff did "not have a documented history of academic achievement below expectations that would support a diagnosis of a learning disability" and noted that "[a]verage, or even slightly below average, is not disabled for purposes of the ADA."

Judge Surrick then paints the picture of Jonathan Love's circumstance in a similar hue:

> Plaintiff's academic history is remarkably similar to that discussed in *Gonzales*. There is no suggestion beyond a few notations made on elementary school reports cards that Plaintiff was disruptive or that he displayed any of the symptoms that are consistent with a finding of ADHD. He did not seek additional help or formal accommodations for ADHD or a learning disability in high school even when faced with classes that required significant amounts of reading involving difficult texts. He never sought to take advantage of the formal accommodations available to students with learning disabilities at his undergraduate institution, nor did he attempt to secure accommodations throughout his graduate studies. Dr. Brunn's testimony suggests that Plaintiff may have some difficulty reading. Nevertheless, his reading impairment does not substantially limit his ability to read and learn as compared to the average person or most people as is required under the ADA.

In a footnote, Judge Surrick comes across as even more emphatic about his view that Mr. Love was not impaired. While the standard the judge

applied was based on the EEOC regulations regarding the major life activity of learning (whereby the "average person standard" holds sway), he said
he would rule the same even if he used the more relativistic standards the
EEOC issued for work activities. He wrote, "We would reach the same
conclusion if we applied the EEOC definition of substantial limitation
found in the regulations dealing with the major life activity of working.
That definition provides that substantial limitation means 'significantly restricted ... as compared to the average person having comparable training,
skills and abilities.'" As far as Judge Surrick was concerned, Jonathan Love
did not qualify as disabled under the ADA regardless of the metric in play.
In the final line of the ruling, he summarized his rationale for denying
Mr. Love's request for accommodations:

> Given all of the evidence presented, including Plaintiff's test scores, clinical
> evaluations, educational history, and his reported ability to function in both
> academic and professional environments, we are not persuaded that Plaintiff
> has a disability as defined under the ADA. Accordingly, we will deny his request
> for injunctive relief in the form of an accommodation on the LSAT and enter
> judgment in favor of Defendant.

The central tenet underlying Judge Surrick's opinion shines through with
pristine clarity: Under the Americans with Disabilities Act, an individual can
only be considered disabled if, in a major life activity, he or she functions
abnormally relative to most people. Jonathan Love was not judged legally
disabled because he functioned at least as well as the average person in the
population. While he might have preferred to function even better, while he
might not always have been able to show what Mr. Wolinsky described as
his "true abilities," while he might even have warranted a clinical diagnosis
in the eyes of some clinicians, he was not impaired when judged against the
standard set by the average person.

That bright line of disability demarcation, drawn initially by the EEOC in
1991 and reinforced in a string of legal decisions over the years, has become
even clearer in the months since Judge Surrick issued his Final Order. At the
beginning of 2008, the federal court in Louisville, Kentucky, issued an opinion in the case of *Jenkins* v. *National Board of Medical Examiners*. That opinion
represents a strongly-worded endorsement of the "average person standard"
and the predominance of impairment over diagnosis in the determination of
disability. In this case, a Judge John G. Heyburn agreed with clinicians that
the medical student, Kirk Jenkins, suffered from a reading disorder that
"unquestionably made it more difficult for Jenkins to keep up with a rigorous
medical school curriculum and to succeed on written tests where he is under

time constraints ..." The judge further observed that "it is a testament to Jenkins' effort and determination that he has done as well as he has in the demanding field he has chosen."

Having accepted that Mr. Jenkins met diagnostic criteria for a reading disorder, the judge indicated that "all of these observations [of slow reading] are not dispositive for the particular purposes of the ADA." According to Judge Heyburn, "Once a person proves he is impaired in some way, he must then prove that the impairment limits a major life activity, and does so substantially." He then invoked the guidance of the Supreme Court in characterizing a major life activity as one that is "of central importance to daily life." He also re-affirmed the principle that "the relevant comparison for purposes of determining disability is to 'most people,' not to one's own hypothetical unimpaired condition or to a chosen subset of one's peers, e.g., medical students."

The judge next made a distinction that is relatively new on the judicial scene for ADA-related cases in higher education: He identified reading as the major life activity under consideration, not test taking, per se. According to the judge, an individual whose limitations were circumscribed to problems with timed test would not be protected under the ADA because test taking, unlike reading considered more broadly, is not "of central importance to daily life." Therefore, the question under consideration for this judge was whether Mr. Jenkins was impaired in reading to such an extent that he could not perform tasks central to daily living. According to the opinion, neither Mr. Jenkins nor his expert witnesses were able to prove to the judge that level of reading impairment. In the judge's words:

> Yet when asked about activities seemingly more "central to most people's daily lives" such as reading the newspaper, reading a label on a food container, reading a menu in a restaurant, or reading correspondence from his attorney, Jenkins indicated that he was amply capable of doing so, albeit more slowly than others ... Lacy [an expert witness] indicated that the adversities experienced by Jenkins were entirely a function of his choice "to pursue a higher education," not a function of the demands of the daily life of most people. There is ample evidence that Jenkins processes written words slowly, and that this condition prevents him from succeeding where success is measured by one's ability to read under time pressure. But Jenkins' inability to identify meaningful "tasks central to most people's daily lives" that he is precluded from performing due to his condition must be fatal to his claim of disability under the ADA.

The judge even cited the amount of time Jenkins requested for accommodations (time-and-one-half) as an indication that he was not substantially impaired "since one who was truly 'substantially limited' in his ability to read seemingly would need significantly more than time-and-a-half to successfully process the undoubtedly complex and technical information on the USMLE [medical board examination]." By Judge Heyburn's construal of the law, it is challenging to conjure any situation whereby a student in higher education could qualify as disabled based on a learning disability or ADHD.

While the Jenkins case might represent a more conservative take on the definition of disability, it by no means stands alone in the context of recent decisions (or, for that matter, most past ones). Another opinion that makes the distinction between diagnosis and disability even more forcefully was issued by the United States District Court for the District of Columbia in the case of *Carolyn Singh* v. *George Washington University School of Medicine and Health Sciences*. Ms. Singh was a medical student who was dismissed from the program for academic reasons. Between the time the dean told her she was being dismissed and her receipt of the formal letter, she sought an evaluation for learning disabilities. A clinical psychologist, Anne C. Newman, Ph.D., concluded that Ms. Singh suffered from a reading disability and a "mild disorder of processing speed." She recommended double time on examinations, use of a reader for exams who would fill in the answer sheets, tape recordings of lectures, access to professors' or students' notes, and use of a laptop for essay exams. Ms. Singh brought the lawsuit against her medical school because the dean held firm in his decision to dismiss her, notwithstanding Dr. Newman's clinical findings.

In his decision, Judge Royce C. Lamberth focused on whether Ms. Singh's problems reading rose to the level of a disability as defined by the ADA. While he accepted that she might have suffered from a disorder, he was less sure that her impairment was "substantial" as defined by the Supreme Court. He reminded the parties that "a mere diagnosis is not sufficient to establish a disability under the ADA." His opinion was designed to assess the evidence for substantial impairment in a major life activity.

Judge Lamberth's impression of Ms. Singh's academic history could easily have been lifted from many of the reviews that my fellow consultants and I have written over the years about other high-functioning examinees seeking accommodations:

> Plaintiff's own experience is replete with academic successes. She performed extremely well in high school and college. While she claims that she consistently performs much lower on multiple-choice tests than on other types of assessments, this Court does not find that she presented sufficient evidence to support that claim. Plaintiff's evidence of the claimed discrepancy is overwhelmingly anecdotal and based solely on her memory of events that occurred years prior. Ms. Singh describes a small number of tests and results, but does

not offer sufficient data to establish a consistent pattern of performance over the years of her formal education. If she has an impairment that substantially interferes with test-taking, multiple-choice or otherwise, this Court would expect such interference to consistently appear throughout similar academic environments. Her recent failures in medical school, and the relatively poor performance on some tests prior to medical school, have not been shown to be the result of her impairment.

The judge next engages in a level of analysis familiar to clinicians and documentation reviewers alike. He reviews alternate explanations that might account for any vagaries in Ms. Singh's academic performance. This consideration of "rule-outs" is essential to settling on a firm diagnosis. The judge describes his thinking as follows:

> This Court does not find that Ms. Singh is substantially limited by impairment even as to the specific activity of multiple choice test taking. Rather, many reasons might explain why she has done relatively poorly on extremely time-limited tests. Perhaps she feels undue pressure that makes it difficult to concentrate on complex concepts. Perhaps she finds herself unable to pay attention to detail and avoid making errors in marking her answer sheet. Perhaps her involvement in extra-curricular activities prevented her from dedicating sufficient time and energy to her studies. Perhaps she does not study well, and simply does not know the material, but is better able to conceal that fact in other testing formats. Ms. Singh even testified that she learned how to get partial credit for books that she had not read by simply repeating things she had learned in the class discussion. Perhaps those same skills worked for her on other testing formats except timed multiple choice, which has no concept of partial credit. Finally, another possible explanation is that Ms. Singh was depressed. This Court previously noted that depression may sometimes be recognized as a disability for purposes of the ADA. Plaintiff, however, offered no evidence that her poor performance was due to depression, and in fact disputed whether she was ever depressed.

Because both the plaintiff and defendants took issue with aspects of Judge Lamberth's decision, Ms. Singh's petition was appealed by both the plaintiffs and defendants to the United States Court of Appeals. That three-judge panel issued a twelve-page decision that affirmed certain of the lower court's findings but contradicted others. They first overturned Judge Lamberth's pre-trial decision regarding the proper method for establishing substantial impairment:

> The district court held that "an ADA plaintiff can be substantially limited based on comparisons of her success to others of comparable age and educational background." Thus "medical students, while in medical school, can

only compare their test scores to their fellow students." GW argues that the proper standard is whether Singh's limitation is substantial as compared to the average person in the general population. We agree with GW.

The appellate court, in analyzing Supreme Court decisions, found that "average person standard" to be the applicable metric for judging Ms. Singh's case. They argued that the "comparable-training standard," which would have made other medical students the comparison group, only applied to the major life activity of working, not learning:

> The [Supreme] Court's language suggests a comparison to the general population, rather than to persons of elite ability or unusual experience. A restriction qualifies as "severe" only if it limits the impaired individual in the context of what "most people" do in their "daily lives."

They further point out the slippery slope inherent in what I have often described as the "You Are as Disabled as the Company You Keep" approach to assessing impairment:

> Finally, we note that any measure of substantial limitation that might change based on a plaintiff's particular educational environment–e.g., a comparison of "medical students ... to their fellow students" would make disabled status vary with a plaintiff's current career choices, and would fail to achieve the ADA's additional purpose of providing "clear, strong, consistent, [and] enforceable standards" to address discrimination.

The judges also acknowledge the inherent frustration for those who might not always live up to their presumed potential. They recognize the realities that not every individual is able to reach the pinnacle of professional achievement:

> It is intuitively appealing to measure limitation by comparing the plaintiff's condition impaired with her own condition, unimpaired. There is something poignant, in some cases even tragic, in the plight of a person cut off from exceptional achievement by some accident of birth or history. But the ADA is not addressed to that plight. Rather, it is designed to enable the disabled, as a group, to participate in mainstream society.

Finally, the judges point out that the average person standard "is currently the law in all of our sister circuits to have addressed the matter." From their perspective, its frequent endorsement in multiple jurisdictions reflects a consensus of opinion that Judge Lamberth should not have ignored. In overturning that aspect of the original decision, the appellate judges added their voice to many others who argue for a standard that can be applied universally.

After years of uncertainty about where to draw the lines in evaluating high-functioning individuals for ADA accommodations, those involved in disability determinations can now benefit from playing on a field that is better demarcated. The clear message emanating from courtrooms across the country is that someone is disabled only if he or she is abnormal relative to most people. While some may not agree with that standard, it has become the standard nonetheless.

Or has it? Just as I was writing this section, feeling good that the light of clarity had finally shone upon an issue that had for so long been clouded by uncertainty, I received an e-mail from the general counsel for a major testing organization. She informed me that two congressional committees had approved a report supporting HR 3195, the "ADA Amendments Act of 2008." The bill itself is posted at http://thomas.loc.gov/home/gpoxmlc110/h3195_rh.xml. The report that accompanies the bill indicates that the purpose of the bill is "to restore the intention and protections of the Americans with Disabilities Act of 1990, providing a clear and comprehensive national mandate for the elimination of discrimination on the basis of disability." HR 3195 is specifically intended to lower the bar for what defines a disability:

> In a departure from the standards enunciated by the U.S. Supreme Court in *Toyota Motor Manufacturing, Kentucky, Inc. v. Williams*, the bill defines "substantially limits" as "materially restricts," which is intended to be a less stringent standard to meet than the Court's interpretation of the definition as "prevents or severely restricts." The bill also explicitly rejects the Court requirement that the terms "substantially" and "major" need "to be interpreted strictly to create a demanding standard for qualifying as disabled." Instead, the bill provides that the definition of disability shall be construed broadly.

The proposed legislation takes dead aim at the string of court decisions that have denied disability status to high-functioning individuals in postsecondary education:

> The Committee also seeks to clarify how the bill's concept of "materially restricts" should be applied for individuals with specific learning disabilities who are frequently substantially limited in the major life activities of learning, reading, writing, thinking, or speaking. In particular, some courts have found that students who have reached a high level of academic achievement are not to be considered individuals with disabilities under the ADA, as such

individuals may have difficulty demonstrating substantial limitation in the major life activities of learning or reading relative to "most people." When considering the condition, manner or duration in which an individual with a specific learning disability performs a major life activity, it is critical to reject the assumption that an individual who performs well academically or otherwise cannot be substantially limited in activities such as learning, reading, writing, thinking, or speaking. As such, the Committee rejects the findings in *Price* v. *National Board of Medical Examiners, Gonzales* v. *National Board of Medical Examiners,* and *Wong* v. *Regents of University of California.*

The Committee believes that the comparison of individuals with specific learning disabilities to "most people" is not problematic unto itself, but requires a careful analysis of the method and manner in which an individual's impairment limits a major life activity. For the majority of the population, the basic mechanics of reading and writing do not pose extraordinary lifelong challenges; rather, recognizing and forming letters and words are effortless, unconscious, automatic processes. Because specific learning disabilities are neurologically-based impairments, the process of reading for an individual with a reading disability (e.g., dyslexia) is word-by-word, and otherwise cumbersome, painful, deliberate and slow—throughout life. The Committee expects that individuals with specific learning disabilities that substantially limit a major life activity will be better protected under the amended Act.

If H.R. 3195 had become law, it would have had a profound impact on the accommodations process. Under that construal of disability, accommodations could flow to anyone who claimed that his high achievement came despite reading that was "cumbersome, painful, deliberate and slow." In many respects, the committee endorsed the argument that Mr. Wolinsky made in his opening statement when he said that Jonathan Love was disabled because he had to work harder than most to achieve as well as he did. Of course, research has established that most college students feel they work harder than others.

It turns out that, over the months since I first learned about the ADA Restoration Act, H.R. 3195 morphed into H.R. 3406 and became the "ADA Amendments Act of 2008." President George Bush signed it into law on September 25, 2008 (you can read this legislative revision of the ADA at http://frwebgate.access.gpo.gov/cgi-bin/getdoc.cgi?dbname=110_cong_bills&docid=f:s3406enr.txt.pdf). While the stated intent of the new law is still to broaden the definition of what constitutes a disability, it does not replace the term "substantially limits" with "meaningfully restricts." However, Congress did not detail how the definition of "substantially limits" should be changed to allow for a lower standard. Instead it directs the Equal Employment Opportunity Commission (EEOC) to promulgate new guidelines that reflect Congress's intent to establish a less demanding definition of disability. We will all have to await the EEOC's new guidelines and the courts interpretation of them before the impact of the ADA Amendments Act becomes clear.

One line in the new law could forever alter the process by which testing organizations handle applications for ADA accommodations. It says that the "question of whether an individual's impairment is a disability under the ADA should not demand extensive analysis." That language would seem to direct the EEOC to promulgate guidelines that restrict the organization's right to request more than cursory verification of the diagnosis. Conceivably, a one-sentence note from a clinician could be regarded as sufficient documentation of the disability. I am sure it is not lost on the reader that the entire tale of Jonathan Love and the LSAC stands as a stark justification for requiring applicants to supply a reasonable degree of support for the claim of disability. It appears especially reasonable in the case of learning disabilities and ADHD, where metrics for judging impairment are so broadly construed and the opportunity for malingering so ample. Few students seeking advantage would find it hard to find a clinician willing to assign one or both of these diagnoses.

Would Mr. Love's fortunes with the LSAC and Judge Surrick have changed under the construal of disability in the ADA Amendments Act of 2008 or even the more lenient "materially restricts" standard that almost worked its way through Congress? I have no idea. It would remain the case that Mr. Love progressed normally throughout his life and across the breadth of his experience. His academic achievements were well in line with his general intellectual abilities. Aside from his self-report and dubious results from a reading test of uncertain validity, Jonathan Love did well for himself and without having to struggle any more than most of us struggle as we wend our way through the challenges of higher education. The decision might therefore still hold in this particular case because he was unable to produce any evidence of a limitation, "substantial" or "material."

Judge Surrick's opinion in the case of *Love* v. *LSAC*, although formed under a legal interpretation of the original ADA, contains a section not incompatible with a less strict construal of the average person standard. He wrote:

> Plaintiff responds that it is inappropriate to depend on quantitative outcomes alone in determining whether a disability exists. Rather, it is the manner in which the outcomes are achieved that is determinative of a disability. The definition of disability based on outcomes alone, particularly when dealing with

learning disabilities, would prevent the court from making a finding of disability in the case of an individual who is extremely bright and hardworking.

We agree that outcomes alone should not be determinative. However, if Plaintiffs IQ was 140 and he scored within the average range on standardized tests and the LSAT, the suggestion that a learning disability was the cause would have more credence.

It would seem that Judge Surrick would leave the door open for granting accommodations to someone with an extremely high IQ who earned an average score on the LSAT. Even though such an individual functioned academically better than most people, he could perhaps be granted extra time if it could be shown that he struggled at all with reading. Judge Surrick, along with the committee endorsing HR 3195, would seem to consider the possibility that the ADA should protect the geniuses amongst us from a degree of underachievement.

And perhaps they should. Maybe our society enjoys a net gain when it gives an advantage to certain segments of the population, even if those citizens might not meet strict standards for eligibility. Perhaps the rest of us are fine with a measure of unfairness in the system if we all benefit over the long term from tilting the field in favor of some. In reality, all laws are embodiments of social policy. The ADA instantiated the social policy our country established for protecting the rights of the disabled. But social policies are mutable, witness current efforts to redraft the legislation. For me, with my visceral abhorrence to anything that smacks of being unfair or elitist, that policy should focus on fairness to all, both in treatment and outcome, rather than advantage to a few. Society at large might have different ideas in mind.

Many months have passed since the issuance of Judge Surrick's decision. From what I gather, it is now regarded as one of the more important ADA-related cases on record. It is also one of the few cases that actually went to a full trial.

Some aspects of this trial will forever mystify me. Why did an organization as prestigious and successful as the DRA take this case all the way to trial? How is it that they did not pull out when they learned of Love's admission to four law schools? Or when they realized that his credibility was easily shaken by hard evidence? Or when they heard their own witness, Dr. Van Auken, support the contention that Mr. Love was not substantially impaired under the ADA? Why would Jonathan Love, an erstwhile lawyer whom his mother describes as a "very private person" allow his personal life to be forever on display in federal case law, on the Web, and in newspapers across the country? Were the lawyers so confident that they advised him to waive the option to keep the testimony confidential? I was so baffled by these kinds of questions that I actually wrote Mr. Wolinsky after the trial. He did not respond.

What has struck me about this case from the outset is how perfectly it illustrates all the many issues inherent in ADA-related disputes in higher education. To me, the most essential lessons address the importance of diagnostic rigor. That three clinicians assigned an ADHD diagnosis to someone as thoroughly competent as Jonathan Love is unfortunate. Had one of them acted less as an advocate and more as a diligent and objective evaluator, I would never have spent the fall of 2006 reading stacks of affidavits, legal declarations, academic records, and application materials. Jonathan Love would have learned that psychiatric diagnosis is not about helping someone gain an advantage. He might have been told that the purpose of assigning a diagnosis is to help an individual with substantial problems receive appropriate treatment.

From my vantage point, Ms. Leopold-Leventhal had it just right when she told the reporter for the *Legal Intelligencer*, "All along, we felt that we were the ones representing the rights of the disabled." When individuals with the mildest of inabilities are regarded as entitled to accommodations and special services, those with significant disabilities become disadvantaged. They lose accessibility to resources; they lose public confidence in the legitimacy of their disorder; they lose the sense that having a disability is regarded by society as serious business.

What did Jonathan Love lose because clinicians were quick to pull the diagnostic trigger? I am not at all sure. For all I know, he was perfectly comfortable carrying a psychiatric diagnosis. He might even have been a bit less anxious knowing that he could use stimulants for test-taking (if he indeed took them). He certainly derived an advantage from getting extra time to take the timed GMAT. When he was not admitted to preferred law schools, he knew he had an option to improve his odds by pursuing extra time on the LSAT. I assume that the trial itself cost him little beyond perhaps a measure of dignity.

And now to the questions surely on the reader's mind: What happened to Jonathan Love? Did he make it into law school? If so, was it a program that he considered befitting what he called his "academic profile"? Was Mr. Wolinsky correct that his client would suffer if he could not take the LSAT with extended time? Was it the LSAC who had it right when they contended Jonathan Love was a perfectly capable student?

Alas, I have little information to report other than what Mr. Love broadcasts on his personal web page. The good news, and it indeed is good news, is that he gained admission to a first tier law school in his home state of

Louisiana, despite his unaccommodated LSAT score. I imagine that his graduate school stint helped his cause considerably. Whether he receives any accommodations in law school is an open question. Because he never required disability services in college or graduate school, I assume he is managing the rigors of his legal education without special assistance. Regardless, he looks to be well on his way toward achieving his goal of becoming an attorney.

Mr. Love's acceptance to an elite law school based, at least in part, on LSAT scores earned under standard test conditions speaks volumes about the legitimacy of the LSAC's position. It stands as a vindication against charges that this testing organization somehow endeavored to deny a person with a disability a necessary accommodation that was deserved under law. Predictions that his purported weaknesses in his capacity to learn and fend off distractions would limit his access to educational opportunities were obviously false. His admission to law school along with his ability to manage the program represent proof positive that the LSAC (and its consultants) had it right. Despite all the concerns that Mr. Love, his mother, lawyers, and psychologists harbored that he would be unable to perform well enough on reading tasks to achieve his goals, the defendants' assessment that he had normal abilities proved accurate. This documentation review process worked as intended.

Can we assume that the federal court system has heard the last of Jonathan Love as a plaintiff filing suit under the Americans with Disabilities Act? I would imagine so. The outcome of his case against the LSAC likely would not encourage him to pursue similar actions in the future, even now that the law has been amended. The new legislation maintains the "average person standard" and the "substantially limits" requirement for the definition of disability. Nonetheless, Mr. Love must pass the bar examination before he can begin practicing as an attorney. Should we all pray he passes the bar on his first attempt?

Resources

The following books, articles, and case citations provide in-depth information about topics covered in this book. While this list is by no means exhaustive, it does offer good starting points for further exploration.

THE AMERICANS WITH DISABILITIES ACT (ADA)

Colker, R., & Milani, A. A. (2005). *The law of disability discrimination.* (5th ed.). Newark, NJ: LexisNexis.

Gordon, M. & Keiser, S., eds. (1998). *Accommodations in higher education under the Americans with Disabilities Act (ADA): A no-nonsense guide for clinicians, educators, administrators, and lawyers.* New York: Guilford Publications and GSI Publications.

Gordon, M., Lewandowski, L., Murphy, K., & Dempsey, K. (2002). ADA-based accommodations in higher education: A survey of clinicians about documentation requirements and diagnostic standards. *Journal of Learning Disabilities, 35,* 357–63.

Lehman, A. F., Alexopoulos, G. S., Goldman, H., Jeste, D., & Ustun, B. (2002). Mental disorders and disability: Time to reevaluate the relationship? In: D. J. Kupfer, M. B. First, D. A. Regier (eds.), *A research agenda for DSM-V* (201–18). Washington, DC: American Psychiatric Association.

Lerner, C. (2004). "Accommodations" for the learning disabled: A level playing field or affirmative action for elites? *Vanderbilt Law Review, 57,* 1041–1122.

Lovett, B. J., Gordon, M., & Lewandowski, L. J. (2009). Measuring impairment in a legal context: Practical considerations in the evaluation of psychiatric and learning disabilities. In: S. Goldstein & J. A. Naglieri (eds), *Assessment of Impairment: From theory to practice.* New York: Springer.

Phillips, S. E. (2002). Legal issues affecting special populations in large-scale test-ing programs. In: G. Tindal & T. M. Haladyna (eds.), *Large-scale assessment programs for all students: Validity, technical adequacy, and implementation* (109–48). Mahwah, NJ: Erlbaum.

Ranseen, J. D., & Parks, G. S. (2005). Test accommodations for postsecondary students: The quandary resulting from the ADA's disability definition. *Psychology, Public Policy, & Law, 11*, 83–108.

ATTENTION DEFICIT HYPERACTIVITY DISORDER (ADHD) IN ADULTS

Barkley, R. A., Murphy, K. R., & Fischer, M. (2008). *ADHD in adults: What the science says.* New York: Guilford.

Frazier, T. W., Youngstrom, E. A., Glutting, J. J., & Watkins, M. W. (2007). ADHD and achievement: Meta-analysis of the child, adolescent, and adult literatures and a concomitant study with college students. *Journal of Learning Disabilities, 40*, 49–65.

Gordon, M., Murphy, K., & Keiser, S. (1998). Attention deficit hyperactivity disorder (ADHD) and test accommodations. *The Bar Examiner, 67(4)*, 26–36.

Gordon, M. & McClure, F. D. (2008). *The down and dirty guide to adult ADHD.* NY: GSI Publications.

Lewandowski, L. J., Lovett, B., Codding, R. S., & Gordon, M. (2008). Symptoms of ADHD and academic concerns in college students with and without ADHD diagnoses. *Journal of Attention Disorders, 12(2)*, 156–61.

Murphy, K. R. and Gordon, M. (2006). The assessment of ADHD in adults. A chapter in: R. A. Barkley (ed). *Attention deficit hyperactivity disorders: A handbook for clinicians—Third Edition.* New York: Guilford Publications.

Nigg, J. T. (2006). *What causes ADHD? Understanding what goes wrong and why.* New York: Guilford Press.

LEARNING DISABILITIES IN ADULTS

Flanagan, D. P., Keiser, S., Bernier, J. E., & Ortiz, S. O. (2003). *Diagnosis of learning disability in adulthood.* Boston: Allyn & Bacon.

Gregg, N., Hoy, C., & Gay, A. F., eds. (1996). *Adults with learning disabilities: Theoretical and practical perspectives.* New York: Guilford Press.

Hughes, C. A., & Smith, J. O. (1990). Cognitive and academic performance of college students with learning disabilities: A synthesis of the literature. *Learning Disability Quarterly, 13*, 66–79.

Wolf, L. E., Schreiber, H. E., & Wasserstein, J., eds. (2008). *Adult learning disorders: Contemporary Issues.* New York: Psychology Press.

RESEARCH ON TEST TAKING

Bolt, S. E., & Thurlow, M. L. (2004). Five of the most frequently allowed testing accommodations in state policy. *Remedial and Special Education*, *25*, 141–52.

Burns, E. (1998). *Test accommodations for students with disabilities*. Springfield, IL: Charles C. Thomas.

Goh, D. S. (2004). *Assessment accommodations for diverse learners*. Boston: Pearson.

Gordon, M., Lewandowski, L., and Keiser, S. (1999). The LD label for relatively well-functioning students: A critical analysis. *Journal of Learning Disabilities*, *32(6)*, 485–90.

Gordon, M. and Murphy, K. (2001). Judging the impact of time limits and distractions on past test performance: A survey of ADHD, clinic-referred, and normal adults. *The ADHD Report*, *9(3)*, 1–5.

Hollenbeck, K. (2002). Determining when test alterations are valid accommodations or modifications for large-scale assessment. In: G. Tindal & T. M. Haladyna (eds.), *Large-scale assessment programs for all students: Validity, technical adequacy, and implementation* (395–425). Mahwah, NJ: Erlbaum.

Kelman, M., & Lester, G. (1997). *Jumping the queue: An inquiry into the legal treatment of students with learning disabilities*. Cambridge, MA: Harvard University Press.

Lewandowski, L. J., Lovett, B. J., Parolin, R., Gordon, M., & Codding, R. S. (2007). Extended time accommodations and the mathematics performance of students with and without ADHD. *Journal of Psychoeducational Assessment*, *25*, 17–28.

Lewandowski, L. J., Lovett, B. J., & Rogers, C. L. (2008). Extended time as a testing accommodation for students with reading disabilities: Does a rising tide lift all ships? *Journal of Psychoeducational Assessment*, *26*, 315–24.

Phillips, S. E. (1994). High-stakes testing accommodations: Validity versus disabled rights. *Applied Measurement in Education*, *7*, 93–120.

Sireci, S. G., Scarpati, S. E., & Li, S. (2005). Test accommodations for students with disabilities: An analysis of the interaction hypothesis. *Review of Educational Research*, *75*, 457–90.

Thurlow, M. L., Thompson, S. J., & Lazarus, S. S. (2006). Considerations for the administration of tests to special needs students: Accommodations, modifications, and more. In: S. M. Downing & T. M. Haladyna (eds.), *Handbook of test development* (pp. 653–673). Mahwah, NJ: Erlbaum.

Zuriff, G. E. (2000). Extra examination time for students with learning disabilities: An examination of the maximum potential thesis. *Applied Measurement in Education*, *13*, 99–117.

IDENTIFICATION OF MALINGERING/DIMINISHED EFFORT

Boone, K. B., ed. (2007). *Assessment of feigned cognitive impairment: A neuropsychological perspective*. New York: Guilford.

Bush, S. S., Ruff, R. M., Tröster, A. I., Barth, J. T., Koffler, S. P., Pliskin, N. H., et al. (2005). Symptom validity assessment: Practice issues and medical necessity. *Archives of Clinical Neuropsychology, 20*, 419–26.

Harrison, A. G. (2006, August). Adults faking ADHD: You must be kidding! *ADHD Report, 14(4)*, 1–7.

Harrison, A. G., Edwards, M. J., & Parker, K. C. H. (2007). Identifying students faking ADHD: Preliminary findings and strategies for detection. *Archives of Clinical Neuropsychology, 22*, 577–88.

Harrison, A. G., Edwards, M. J., & Parker, K. C. (2008). Identifying students feigning dyslexia: Preliminary findings and strategies for detection. *Dyslexia, (14)*, 228–246.

Jachimowicz, G., & Geiselman, R. E. (2004). Comparison of ease of falsification of attention deficit hyperactivity disorder diagnosis using standard behavioral rating scales. *Cognitive Science Online, 2*, 6–20.

Mittenberg W., Patton C., Canyock E., & Condit D. (2002). Base rates of malingering and symptom exaggeration. *Journal of Clinical and Experimental Neuropsycholog, (24)*, 1094–1102.

Osmon, D. C., Plambeck, E., Klein, L., & Mano, Q. (2006). The Word Reading Test of Effort in adult learning disability: A simulation study. *The Clinical Neuropsychologist, 20*, 315–24.

Pankratz, L., & Binder, L. M. (1997). Malingering on intellectual and neuropsychological measures. In: R. Rogers (ed.), *Clinical assessment of malingering and deception* (2nd ed., 223–36). New York: Guilford.

Ranseen, R. D. (1998). Lawyers with ADHD: The special test accommodation controversy. *Professional Psychology Research and Practice, (29)*, 450–459.

Sullivan, B. K., May, K., & Galbally, L. (2007). Symptom exaggeration by college adults in attention-deficit hyperactivity disorder and learning disorder assessments. *Applied Neuropsychology, 14*, 189–207.

COURT CASES RELEVANT TO ADA CONSIDERATIONS IN HIGHER EDUCATION

Bartlett v. *N. Y. State Bd. of Law Examiners*, 226 F.3d 69, 81–82 (2d Cir.2000).

Gonzales v. *National Board of Medical Examiners*, 225 F.3d 620, 627 (6th Cir.2000).

Jenkins v. *National Board of Medical Examiners*, 2008 U.S. Dist., WL 410237.

Krolik v. *National Board of Medical Examiners*. 2006 U.S. Dist. LEXIS 44561 (D. Ariz., 2006)

Love v. *Law School Admission Counsel, Inc.*, F. Supp.2d, 2007 WL 737785, 34 NDLR P 120, E. D. Pa., March 09, 2007 (NO. 06-CV-3333)

Powell v. *National Board of Medical Examiners*, 364 F.3d 79, 88 (2d Cir.2004)

Price v. *National Board of Medical Examiners*, 966 F. Supp. 419 (S.D. W. Va. 1997).

Shamonsky v. *St. Luke's School of Nursing et al.* (Pennsylvania Middle District Court, 2006) Case Number: 3:2006cv01430

Singh v. *George Washington University School of Medicine and Health Sciences*, Civil Action No. 03-1681 (RCL).

Index

About the Author

MICHAEL GORDON, Ph.D. is Chief Clinical Child Psychologist and Director of the ADHD Program in the Department of Psychiatry, at SUNY Upstate Medical University. He is also Director of Child and Adolescent Psychiatric Services, as well as a Professor in the Department of Psychiatry. He is Associate Editor for the journal, *ADHD Report*, and is a reviewer for the *Journal of Learning Disabilities* and the *Journal of Attention Disorders*. Gordon was presented with a Hall of Fame Award by CHADD, Children and Adults with Attention Deficit/Hyperactivity Disorder, a national support group for those with ADHD.